Taxcafe.co.uk Tax Guides

The Big Landlord Tax Increase

How to Beat the Cut in
Mortgage Tax Relief

By Carl Bayley BSc FCA
and
Nick Braun PhD

Important Legal Notices:

Taxcafe®
Tax Guide - "The Big Landlord Tax Increase"

Published by:
Taxcafe UK Limited
67 Milton Road
Kirkcaldy KY1 1TL
Tel: (0044) 01592 560081
Email: team@taxcafe.co.uk

8th edition, July 2020

ISBN 978-1-911020-56-1

Trademarks
Taxcafe® is a registered trademark of Taxcafe UK Limited. All other trademarks, names and logos in this tax guide may be trademarks of their respective owners.

Disclaimer
Before reading or relying on the content of this tax guide please read the disclaimer carefully.

Disclaimer

1. This guide is intended as **general guidance** only and does NOT constitute accountancy, tax, investment or other professional advice.

2. The authors and Taxcafe UK Limited make no representations or warranties with respect to the accuracy or completeness of this publication and cannot accept any responsibility or liability for any loss or risk, personal or otherwise, which may arise, directly or indirectly, from reliance on information contained in this publication.

3. Please note that tax legislation, the law and practices of Government and regulatory authorities (e.g. HM Revenue & Customs) are constantly changing. We therefore recommend that for accountancy, tax, investment or other professional advice, you consult a suitably qualified accountant, tax advisor, financial adviser, or other professional adviser.

4. Please also note that your personal circumstances may vary from the general examples provided in this guide and your professional adviser will be able to provide specific advice based on your personal circumstances.

5. This guide covers UK taxation only and any references to 'tax' or 'taxation', unless the contrary is expressly stated, refer to UK taxation only. Please note that references to the 'UK' do not include the Channel Islands or the Isle of Man. Foreign tax implications are beyond the scope of this guide.

6. All persons described in the examples in this guide are entirely fictional. Any similarities to actual persons, living or dead, or to fictional characters created by any other author, are entirely coincidental.

7. The views expressed in this publication are the authors' own personal views and do not necessarily reflect the views of any organisation which they may represent.

About the Authors & Taxcafe

Carl Bayley is the author of a series of Taxcafe guides designed specifically for the layman. Carl's particular speciality is his ability to take the weird, complex and inexplicable world of taxation and set it out in the kind of clear, straightforward language taxpayers themselves can understand. As he often says himself, "my job is to translate 'tax' into English".

In addition to being a recognised author, Carl has often spoken about taxation on radio and television, including the BBC's *It's Your Money* programme and the Jeremy Vine Show on Radio 2.

A chartered accountant by training, Carl is a former Chairman of the Tax Faculty of the Institute of Chartered Accountants in England and Wales and a member of the Institute's governing Council.

Nick Braun founded Taxcafe.co.uk in 1999, along with his partner, Aileen Smith. As the driving force behind the company, their aim is to provide affordable plain-English tax information to private individuals, investors, business owners and professional advisors.

Since then Taxcafe has become one of the best-known tax publishers in the UK and has won several business awards.

Nick has been involved in the tax publishing world since 1989 as a writer, editor and publisher. He holds a doctorate in economics from the University of Glasgow, where he was awarded the prestigious William Glen Scholarship and later became a Research Fellow. Prior to that, he graduated with distinction from the University of South Africa, the country's oldest university, earning the highest results in economics in the university's history.

Contents

Introduction

Back in 2015, former Chancellor of the Exchequer George Osborne dropped a huge tax bombshell on landlords.

He announced that tax relief on interest and other finance costs paid by residential landlords would be phased out over a period of four years. In its place landlords would receive a '20% tax reduction'.

The tax relief cuts started in 2017 and, from 6th April 2020 onwards, residential landlords no longer receive 40% or 45% tax relief on their interest payments. As a result, many will see the Income Tax they pay each year rise by thousands of pounds.

The way the change has been designed also means many landlords who were previously basic-rate taxpayers will now pay tax at 40% and some landlords face other tax stings including loss of their child benefit and Income Tax personal allowance and having to pay the 45% additional rate on some of their income.

In this guide, we explain how the tax relief restriction operates and what you can do to protect yourself from a much bigger tax bill.

This latest edition has also been fully updated throughout to take account of how the current coronavirus crisis is affecting landlords and the action they can take to save tax in the current climate.

In Chapters 1 and 2 we provide a brief overview of the changes and explain why we think the Government has been hammering landlords.

In Chapters 3 and 4 we look at which types of property investor and which types of finance costs are affected by the change.

In Chapter 5 we explain the complexities of the new 20% tax reduction and the circumstances in which it is restricted.

Chapters 6 and 7 contain case studies showing how different landlords are likely to be affected by the reduction in their tax relief – in general but also this year specifically in light of the coronavirus crisis.

As you will see, some landlords will come away relatively unscathed, others will suffer a catastrophic drop in income.

Chapter 8 contains some extra information for Scottish landlords, now their Income Tax rates are set by the Scottish Parliament.

In Chapter 9 we examine how the reduction in tax relief, coupled with changes in interest rates (both up and down) will affect landlords.

In Chapters 10 to 27 we turn to tax planning and explain how landlords can beat the tax increase by:

- Increasing the rent they charge
- Postponing or accelerating tax deductible expenses
- Employing family members
- Accelerating tax relief for finance costs
- Making pension contributions
- Reducing buy-to-let mortgages
- Selling properties
- Managing dividend income (company owners)
- Emigrating
- Investing in other types of property
- Converting properties to a different use
- Using alternative investment structures
- Transferring properties to their spouses/partners
- Using a company (over 30 pages on this key issue)

Finally, in the last chapter we take a look at the 'cash basis' for property businesses, which could make it simpler for landlords to manage their tax affairs, although it also contains *another* potential sting in the tail for those with interest and other finance costs.

It's important to know about the cash basis because you may be forced to use it unless you actively opt out!

Scope of this Guide & Limitations

It is possible that further changes will be announced that affect some of the information contained in this guide.

Although the guide covers a fair amount of ground, it does not cover every possible scenario – that would be impossible without making it much longer and possibly much more difficult to digest. Landlords come in many different shapes and sizes, so it is possible some of the information contained in this guide will not be appropriate to your individual circumstances.

The main focus of this tax guide is *Income Tax* planning, i.e. how the reduction in tax relief for finance costs will affect the Income Tax paid by residential landlords and what they can do about it. Steps you take to reduce one type of tax can have an adverse impact on your liability to pay other taxes.

There are also *non-tax* factors that have to be considered when taking action to reduce your tax bill. In some instances other considerations will outweigh any potential tax savings.

It is therefore vital to obtain professional advice before taking action based on information in this guide. The authors and Taxcafe UK Ltd cannot accept responsibility for any loss that may arise as a consequence of any action taken, or any decision to refrain from taking action, as a result of reading this guide.

Scottish Taxpayers

The Scottish Parliament has the power to set its own Income Tax rates, although it cannot change the personal allowance, or the tax rates on interest or dividend income. In Chapter 8 we explain the key differences.

Despite these differences, the vast majority of the information contained in this guide remains equally relevant to Scottish taxpayers. However, unless stated to the contrary, all examples, tables, calculations and illustrations are based on the assumption the taxpayer concerned is not a Scottish taxpayer.

Landlords who are not Scottish taxpayers, but who invest in property in Scotland, are unaffected by Scottish Income Tax rates.

They do, however, pay Land and Buildings Transaction Tax on property purchases in Scotland (instead of Stamp Duty Land Tax).

Welsh Taxpayers

The Welsh Assembly also has the power to set its own Income Tax rates. However, the rates applying for the current 2020/21 tax year are the same as the main UK rates applying in England and Northern Ireland. The vast majority of the information contained in this guide will again remain equally relevant if and when Welsh taxpayers are subject to different tax rates.

Landlords who are not Welsh taxpayers, but who invest in property in Wales, will be unaffected by any future changes in Welsh Income Tax rates. They do, however, pay Land Transaction Tax on property purchases in Wales (instead of Stamp Duty Land Tax).

Accruals versus Cash

As we will see in Chapter 28, the 'cash basis' is now the 'default' method for most landlords to calculate their tax liabilities. However, despite this, we believe many landlords will generally prefer to continue using the traditional accounting method under generally accepted accounting principles ('GAAP'), also sometimes known as the 'accruals basis', and will therefore opt out of the cash basis.

We will look at the advantages and disadvantages of the cash basis in Chapter 28 and, in particular, its impact on the restrictions in tax relief for interest and finance costs. Throughout the rest of this guide, however, we will assume landlords continue to use the traditional accruals basis. Hence, unless stated to the contrary, all examples, tables, calculations and illustrations are based on the assumption the taxpayer concerned is accounting for their rental income under GAAP.

Spouses and Partners

Any references to a 'spouse' throughout this guide mean a legally married spouse or registered civil partner. Unmarried partners are generally subject to different treatment for tax purposes.

Chapter 1

The Tax Change in a Nutshell

Before the Change

Before the tax change, landlords could generally claim ALL their mortgage interest as a tax deductible business expense.

So if you had £25,000 of rental income, £10,000 of mortgage interest and no other expenses (to keep the example simple) your taxable rental profit would have been £15,000.

As a higher-rate taxpayer you would have paid 40% tax (£6,000) and as a basic-rate taxpayer you would have paid 20% tax (£3,000).

After the Change

For residential landlords, the mortgage interest tax deduction was phased out over a period of four years. From the current 2020/21 tax year onwards, mortgage interest is no longer a tax deductible expense.

In its place residential landlords now receive a basic-rate 'tax reduction'. Essentially what this means is an amount equal to 20% of your interest costs is deducted from your final tax bill. Higher-rate taxpayers previously enjoyed 40% tax relief on their finance costs, so their tax relief has been halved.

For example, if you have £25,000 of rental income, £10,000 of mortgage interest, and no other expenses (again, to keep the example simple), you will now have a taxable rental profit of **£25,000**, not £15,000.

If you are a higher-rate taxpayer you will pay 40% tax on this 'profit' (£10,000) and if you are a basic-rate taxpayer you'll pay 20% tax (£5,000). You will then be given a 'tax reduction' equal to 20% of your interest costs, which in this case is £2,000 (£10,000 x 20%).

So if you're a basic-rate taxpayer, you will still pay £3,000 tax overall and will be unaffected by the change. If you're a higher-rate taxpayer, you'll pay £8,000 tax overall – an increase of £2,000.

By the way, a higher-rate taxpayer is someone with more than £50,000 of total taxable income this year (2020/21); or £43,430 for Scottish taxpayers.

In a Nutshell

If you are a basic-rate taxpayer you will not pay more tax.

If you are a higher-rate taxpayer you can make a rough and ready estimate of how much extra tax you'll pay in 2020/21 and future tax years by multiplying your total finance costs by 20%.

This is because instead of getting 40% tax relief on your finance costs you only get 20% from now on.

Thus, if your total finance costs are £10,000, your tax bill will be £2,000 higher than it would have been if your interest was fully deductible (£10,000 x 20%).

But it's Not Always that Simple

Because you cannot deduct your interest costs from your residential rental income, your total taxable income could be significantly higher than it would have been otherwise.

This means you could end up in a higher tax bracket.

Thus some landlords who were previously always basic-rate taxpayers could end up as higher-rate taxpayers. As a result they could end up paying 40% tax instead of 20%.

In addition, some landlords could see their taxable income go over other key thresholds (for example, £100,000 where the personal allowance is withdrawn or £150,000 where the additional rate of tax is payable).

Some landlords who are higher-rate taxpayers may be only *partially* affected by the tax relief restriction. This will be the case if the amount of income you have taxed at 40% is less than your mortgage interest.

Example

Ruth is a full-time landlord. Her total taxable rental profit is £55,000. This is before deducting her interest costs of £10,000.

If her interest costs were tax deductible, as they were in the past, she would only enjoy 40% tax relief on the first £5,000 (£2,000). This would reduce her taxable income to £50,000 (the higher-rate threshold). She would then enjoy just 20% tax relief on the final £5,000 (£1,000). The total tax relief on her interest costs would thus be £3,000.

In practice, she now only receives 20% tax relief on her interest costs, so her total tax relief is £2,000 (£10,000 x 20%).

The extra tax she pays because of the tax relief restriction is therefore £1,000. This is not 20% of her interest costs (as per the rough and ready estimate outlined above). Instead, it is 20% of the amount by which her taxable income exceeds the higher-rate threshold.

At the risk of overcomplicating matters, we should perhaps modify our rough and ready estimate and say that many higher-rate taxpayers can calculate how much extra tax they will pay in 2020/21 and future tax years by multiplying the *smaller* of these two numbers by 20%:

- Your interest costs
- Your taxable income in excess of the higher-rate threshold

Taxable income includes income from all sources, including your residential rental profit before deducting interest and finance costs.

In Ruth's case, her interest costs are £10,000 and she has £5,000 of taxable income in excess of the higher-rate threshold.

Multiplying the smaller of these two numbers by 20% gives us £1,000 – the amount Ruth's tax bill increases because of the mortgage tax relief restriction.

In Chapter 6 we will take a look at some case studies showing how a variety of landlords are affected by the tax change.

The Current 2020/21 Tax Year

This is the first year the tax relief restriction is in full force. However, many landlords will be more preoccupied with something else: battling the economic fallout from the coronavirus crisis.

Some landlords will be completely unaffected, with properties that are fully occupied and tenants who are paying all their rent.

Others may be experiencing a double whammy of falling income from their main job or business *plus* a fall in rental income from their property business.

Your rental income may have fallen if some of your properties have lain empty for longer than normal (student properties, for example) or if some of your tenants have been unable to pay their rent and the arrears have become irrecoverable bad debts. In some cases landlords may have agreed to waive or reduce rent to help their tenants.

If you expect your total taxable income from all sources to fall below £50,000 this year (the higher-rate threshold) you will be completely unaffected by the mortgage tax relief restriction this year.

If you expect your total taxable income to fall but still be higher than £50,000 then you will still be affected by mortgage tax relief restriction.

In Chapter 7 we will take a look at some case studies showing how a variety of landlords may be affected by the tax change this year specifically.

And in the tax planning chapters that follow we will examine how the coronavirus crisis may affect what action you take this year to reduce your tax bill.

What about the Previous 2019/20 Tax Year?

It's worth mentioning the previous 2019/20 tax year for those who have yet to complete their tax return.

Last year, three quarters (75%) of residential landlords' finance costs were not tax deductible.

If you were a higher-rate taxpayer last year you can make a very rough estimate of how much extra tax you'll pay because of the tax change by multiplying your total finance costs by 15%.

The higher-rate threshold was the same last year as this year: You were a higher-rate taxpayer last year if your taxable income was more than £50,000 (£43,430 for Scottish taxpayers).

Once again it's important to stress this rough and ready estimate cannot be relied on by all higher-rate taxpayers.

If you were a basic-rate taxpayer last year, despite the fact that three quarters of your interest costs were not tax deductible, you will not be affected by the tax change for that year.

Chapter 2

Why Landlords Were Targeted & Future Tax Changes

Former Chancellor George Osborne (the man you should blame for the mortgage tax relief change) staked his reputation on eliminating the UK's Budget deficit, which ballooned after the 2008 financial crisis. Osborne was a 'fiscal conservative' which means he didn't like borrowing money.

However, despite years of 'austerity' Mr Osborne found it very difficult to eliminate the deficit – the Government was continually spending a lot more than it was taking in taxes.

On the tax raising front, the Conservatives tied their own hands by making the following pledge in their 2015 election manifesto:

"A Conservative Government will not increase the rates of VAT, Income Tax or National Insurance in the next Parliament."

As a result, they had to become more creative and tackle the deficit by introducing tax increases via the back door by "tackling tax avoidance and tax planning, evasion and compliance, and imbalances in the tax system".

Allowing landlords to claim tax relief on their mortgage interest was, apparently, one of those 'imbalances'. The 2015 Summer Budget document stated that:

"The current tax system supports landlords over and above ordinary homeowners. Landlords can deduct costs they incur when calculating the tax they pay on their rental income. A large portion of those costs are interest payments on the mortgage. Mortgage Interest Relief was withdrawn from homeowners 15 years ago. However, landlords still receive the relief. The ability to deduct these costs puts investing in a rental property at an advantage."

By likening landlords to homeowners it is clear that those in charge did not view landlords as proper business owners. It is, after all, a fundamental principle of taxation in most of the developed world that businesses can deduct all of their expenses when calculating their taxable profits.

There are some exceptions, for example entertainment spending is generally disallowed because the taxman believes meals at fancy restaurants and the like are more for personal pleasure than for genuine business purposes.

However, interest on loans used to buy business assets that produce taxable income (like rental property) has always been considered a bread and butter 'revenue expense', entitled to full tax relief.

It's Not Fair!

Do landlords run 'proper' businesses? The question doesn't even deserve an answer, as anyone who spends their time managing rental property knows.

Nevertheless, the Government thought the change to mortgage tax relief was 'fair' because it would supposedly target 'wealthier landlords' only:

"Tax relief for finance costs is particularly beneficial for wealthier landlords with larger incomes, as every £1 of finance cost they incur allows them to pay 40p or 45p less tax."

The Government decided to 'rectify' this by giving every landlord tax relief on their finance costs at the basic rate only (i.e. 20%).

But surely if the Government wanted to target wealthy landlords only, it would have imposed higher taxes on those who don't have any mortgages at all? After all, if you own a lot of rental properties but also have a lot of mortgage debt you aren't necessarily wealthy but *aspire* to being wealthy.

Landlords were probably viewed as an easy target because most were enjoying healthy rental profits, thanks to the historically low level of interest rates. The fact that many had also enjoyed healthy capital gains (even if only on paper) meant they couldn't expect much sympathy from their fellow taxpayers.

The fact that landlords were seen as an easy target was further confirmed by the announcement of a 3% increase in the rates of Stamp Duty Land Tax applying to purchases of additional residential property and the failure to extend a cut in Capital Gains Tax to those disposing of residential property.

Apart from the desire to raise tax as sneakily as possible and level the playing field between homeowners and landlords, another reason for the tax change was to protect the banks from going bust again. Attempting to justify the change in the July 2015 Budget the Government stated that:

"The Bank of England has also noted in its recent Financial Stability Report that the rapid growth of buy to let mortgages could pose a risk to the UK's financial stability."

This seems to be a case of shutting the stable door after the horse has bolted. The time to clamp down on mortgage lending was before the 2008 financial crisis, i.e. when the banks were handing out cash hand over fist and offering products like 125% mortgages and self-certified loans (also known as 'liar loans').

Putting landlords under more financial pressure has surely only increased the likelihood of mortgage defaults.

Will the Mortgage Tax Increase Be Reversed?

Although the restriction on landlord interest is deeply unfair, we think it is extremely unlikely there will be any kind of u-turn in the foreseeable future, despite vigorous campaigning by landlord groups.

The Government has been spending vast sums of money to stem the economic damage caused by the covid-19 lockdown, including paying the salaries of millions of 'furloughed' workers and giving cash grants of up to £25,000 to many businesses.

According to some estimates, Government borrowing this year could exceed £300 billion and perhaps even £500 billion if the economy remains very weak. To put that in perspective, borrowing peaked at £158 billion after the financial crisis, a figure that looks somewhat quaint today.

The probability of this landlord tax increase being reversed, when the public purse is under so much pressure, is therefore as close to zero as it could ever be.

Sadly, landlords must always remember any injustices they suffer will rarely attract sympathy from the general public, especially from the small, but vocal, minority, who seem to think all landlords are multi-millionaires, or belong to the landed aristocracy!

Hence, unfortunately, we must all accept the mortgage tax change is probably here to stay for the foreseeable future.

Future Tax Increases

The question that is more relevant now is:

What other tax increases can we expect to pay for the coronavirus crisis?

With interest rates so low at present, the Government may be able get away with borrowing huge sums of money for now – the Government pays just 0.20% per year to borrow money for 10 years.

And the Bank of England is helping the Government by simply printing the money the Government needs to borrow – something considered highly taboo in normal times.

The Governor of the Bank of England, Andrew Bailey, has stated that the bank can help spread the cost of the coronavirus crisis to society over time. He thinks we do not need to live through the same type of austerity that was experienced during the financial crisis (big Government spending cuts and tax increases).

Eventually, however, there will surely have to be a reckoning of some sort. The UK Government will have to reassure the world that it has its financial house in order and, while we may see some tax cuts in the short-term, to help restart the economy, in the longer term this will inevitably mean announcing future tax increases. These tax increases may only be introduced gradually, to avoid snuffing out the economic recovery.

Some of any tax increases will almost certainly target high income earners and those with assets. We can expect politicians to start using that phrase, "it's only fair that those with the broadest shoulders pay a little more," just as they did during the 2008 financial crisis.

Broader tax increases should also be expected. Chancellor Rishi Sunak has already stated that everyone will have to 'chip in' to right the ship.

In their 2019 election manifesto the Conservative Party promised to not increase the rates of income tax, national insurance or VAT. This promise will probably have to be broken, given the extraordinary times we find ourselves in.

Even if the Government doesn't increase these tax rates, there are plenty of other ways it can raise tax, although raising large sums of money will be more difficult.

We at Taxcafe have no idea what shape any such tax increases would take or when they would be introduced. But it's important when planning your tax affairs to keep one eye on possible future tax changes as well.

Possible future tax increases include:

Freezing the Higher-rate Threshold
The higher-rate threshold was £45,000 back in 2017/18 and has increased by more than the rate of inflation to £50,000 today. The Government could therefore argue that freezing the threshold for several years is justifiable.

Freezing tax thresholds is the easiest way for any government to increase taxes without telling anyone.

Increasing the Additional Rate
The additional rate was reduced from 50% to 45% in 2013. Increasing the rate back to 50% would be much easier politically than raising the 20% basic rate or 40% higher rate.

A Penny (or Two) on Income Tax
During the 2019 general election the Liberal Democrats pledged to increase all income tax rates by 1% to raise money for the NHS. They said this would raise £7 billion a year. Such a tax increase would be more politically palatable for a Conservative Government following a health crisis.

Increasing Dividend Tax Rates

Dividend tax rates were increased by 7.5% in 2016 to clamp down on company owners who take most of their income as dividends and pay little or no national insurance.

There would be little sympathy from the wider public if shareholders were once again forced to pay more tax. We wouldn't be surprised to see tax rates increase by 2.5% at some point.

Increasing National Insurance Rates

At present salary earners, sole traders and business partners pay 2% national insurance on income over £50,000. This rate could be increased to help fund the NHS and to help fund other state benefits.

On income below £50,000 self-employed people currently pay 9% national insurance compared with the 12% paid by salary earners. We can expect the rates for self-employed business owners to be brought in line with those of salary earners. Chancellor Rishi Sunak has already hinted this will happen.

Employers also pay an additional 13.8% national insurance on employees' salaries and some commentators even fear the Chancellor might attempt to replicate some or all of this cost for the self-employed as well.

Landlords do not generally pay national insurance on rental income, so should be unaffected by any increases in this tax. This does beg the question whether the Government might consider starting to charge national insurance on rental income. However, this would be a complex issue for them to tackle, as it would mean reclassifying the nature of rental income and rental businesses, and could therefore cost the Government as much in other tax reliefs as it raises in additional national insurance. For this reason, we think such a change is unlikely in the foreseeable future.

Reducing Pension Tax Relief

Higher-rate tax relief on pension contributions is estimated to cost the Government roughly £10 billion per year. For many years now commentators in the pensions industry have feared that it will be taken away and replaced with basic-rate tax relief on all pension contributions.

There were rumours circulating that an announcement would be made in the March 2020 Budget by Sajid Javid, before he resigned as Chancellor of the Exchequer. No changes were announced by the current Chancellor Rishi Sunak.

Scrapping higher-rate tax relief altogether would take away much of the incentive to save into a pension (except for those who also enjoy a contribution from their employer). A far easier change would be to reduce the annual allowance (the amount you can contribute each year) from £40,000 to perhaps £30,000 or £20,000.

Scrapping Entrepreneurs Relief

Entrepreneurs Relief allows you to pay just 10% capital gains tax when you sell your business or wind it up. In the March 2020 Budget the lifetime limit was reduced from £10 million of capital gains to just £1 million. We wouldn't rule out a further reduction or even a complete scrapping of this tax relief.

Increasing Capital Gains Tax

We also wouldn't rule out increases in capital gains tax generally because people with assets are likely to be an easy political target. At present higher-rate taxpayers pay 28% capital gains tax when they sell residential property and 20% when they sell other assets. These rates could be increased significantly at the stroke of a pen.

Inheritance Tax

Changes to inheritance tax have been widely mooted following a report by the rather Orwellian sounding 'Office of Tax Simplification'. However, there was no mention of any changes in the March 2020 Budget.

The inheritance tax nil rate band has been frozen at its current level of £325,000 since 2009. In the absence of a major overhaul of the despised grave robber's tax, the £325,000 exemption could remain frozen for many more years. And because people with significant assets are such an easy political target, it would be easy to introduce a tax rate higher than 40%, perhaps for larger estates.

Stamp Duty Land Tax

And because people who buy lavish homes enjoy no sympathy from their fellow taxpayers, we wouldn't rule out longer-term increases in the stamp duty land tax paid on expensive properties, or an increase in the rate for additional properties (for example, from 3% to 4% like it is in Scotland).

VAT

The Government has frozen the VAT registration threshold at £85,000 until 31ˢᵗ March 2022. The Office of Tax Simplification would like to see a drastic reduction in the threshold on the grounds that a high threshold limits the amount of work small businesses take on. In the absence of any big changes it would be fairly easy to keep the threshold at £85,000 for several more years to gradually drag more businesses into the VAT net.

New Wealth or Property Taxes

Some commentators think we may see a new 'wealth tax' or 'property tax', i.e. an annual charge on individuals with total wealth above a certain threshold, or property worth in excess of a certain value. Such taxes already exist in other countries and we have a model for an annual property tax in the UK already: the Annual Tax on Enveloped Dwellings, or 'ATED'.

ATED currently applies to UK residential property worth over £500,000, held by a company or other 'non-natural person', and not in qualifying business use (luckily, renting property to an unconnected third party is a qualifying business for this purpose). It would be easy for the Government to extend something like ATED to property held by any person, with no exemption for business use. We don't like the idea, but we can't rule it out.

A Final Word on Potential Tax Increases

It's important to stress that all of the above is highly speculative. We do not know what tax changes policymakers have up their sleeves.

We're also not making any moral judgements about whether any such tax increases would be right or wrong. The country's finances will be in a mess when we get through the coronavirus crisis, as will the finances of many taxpayers who may wish to do what they can to protect their families.

Perhaps the only moral issue we are concerned with is that we believe it is wrong to target a particular segment of the population, or a particular business sector, just because it is politically expedient to do so. But that's not the future: we're already there!

Chapter 3

Who is Affected by the Tax Relief Restriction?

Residential Property Letting Businesses

The tax relief restriction affects *residential* property businesses only – commercial property businesses are unaffected by the change, as are furnished holiday letting businesses.

Of course, this is little consolation to the vast majority of small landlords who mostly invest in houses and flats. Investing in commercial property is a whole different ball game, requiring a different skill set.

Nevertheless, many business owners do own their own trading premises (e.g. an office, shop or factory unit) and will be relieved to hear they may continue to claim full tax relief on their mortgage interest.

It is also important to note the tax relief restriction does not just apply to interest on buy-to-let mortgages – it applies to almost all the finance costs incurred by a residential property letting business.

More specifically, the legislation restricts the tax relief on 'dwelling-related loans'. Generally speaking, dwelling-related loans are loans used to generate income from dwelling houses.

So if you take out a loan to buy a car for use in your residential property letting business, the tax relief on your interest payments will be restricted. Similarly, if you take out a loan to buy an office to run your residential property letting business from, the tax relief on your interest payments will be restricted. The fact that the office may be a commercial property is irrelevant – the loan will be treated as a dwelling-related loan because it is for the purpose of generating income from dwelling houses.

The restriction also applies to loan arrangement fees and other finance costs.

Property Developers

The interest restriction does not apply to businesses that develop property for sale or deal in property – it applies only to residential property letting businesses, i.e. businesses that generate income from renting out residential property. In other words, if you borrow money to buy a property with the intention of doing it up and selling it on for a profit, the tax relief on your finance costs will not be restricted.

What is a Dwelling House?

There is no definition of 'dwelling house' in the legislation, so the phrase takes its ordinary meaning. According to HM Revenue and Customs the distinctive characteristic of a dwelling house is its ability to provide the facilities required for day-to-day private domestic existence.

Most landlords who rent out flats and houses earn income from dwelling houses and will therefore have their tax relief restricted.

Nursing homes and hotels that are run as a trade and offer other services are not generally considered to be dwelling houses.

Running a guest house is also usually considered to be a trade. Hence, while interest relief on a loan to buy, or finance, a guest house must be restricted to the proportion of the property used for business purposes, it will not generally be necessary to apply the further restrictions discussed in this guide.

Student accommodation is more of a grey area. Halls of residence owned by universities are generally considered not to be dwelling houses. However, houses in multiple occupation (HMOs) that provide bedrooms and communal kitchens and living rooms are generally considered to be dwelling houses.

Remortgaging

What happens if you borrow against a rental property that you already own? As has always been the case, what matters is how you *use* the money, not how the loan is secured.

For example, let's say you already own a residential property and borrow against it to buy a commercial rental property. You will be entitled to full tax relief on your interest payments, i.e. you are not affected by the tax change.

But if you use the loan to invest in another residential rental property, you are, as you would expect, subject to the tax relief restriction.

And if you use the money for personal reasons, for example to pay your child's school fees, there will generally be no tax relief on the interest payments at all, as has always been the case.

There is an important exception to this rule, however. Tax relief is available when you borrow against a rental property up to its original value when first rented out, no matter what the borrowed funds are used for. Even if the borrowed money is used for personal reasons, the interest still qualifies for tax relief.

For example, let's say you inherit a flat worth £200,000 and begin renting it out. If you then borrow against the property (up to £200,000) all the interest will qualify for tax relief, even if you use the money for personal reasons, for example to pay school fees.

Despite some difficulties for a short period a few years ago, this view is generally accepted by HM Revenue and Customs and, indeed, is now even reflected in their own manuals.

Nonetheless, where the additional funds used for personal reasons are borrowed against a residential rental property, the amount of tax relief is restricted to basic rate only (20%), just as it is for any other dwelling-related loan.

Mixed Properties

What happens if you own a mixed property with both a commercial and residential component, for example a shop with a flat on top? If there is a single loan over the entire property the finance costs have to be apportioned. The interest relating to the shop remains fully tax deductible; interest on the flat is restricted.

Mixed Property Businesses

Complexity may arise where a landlord owns a mixture of commercial and residential properties. Where each property has its own mortgage the calculations are relatively straightforward:

interest relating to commercial properties remains fully tax deductible; interest on residential properties is restricted.

However, an apportionment is required when a single loan facility is used to buy both residential and commercial properties, or where borrowings are used to buy assets for use in the combined business, e.g. cars, equipment and business premises.

Companies Unaffected

The interest relief restrictions for landlords do not apply to companies, so if your residential properties are held inside a company there is generally no restriction to the tax relief the company can claim on its interest payments.

It doesn't matter whether the company carries on the property business directly or in partnership. However, the exemption does not apply where the company carries on the business in a fiduciary or representative capacity (i.e. as a nominee rather than the beneficial owner).

The restrictions do, however, apply to partnerships and limited liability partnerships, as well as certain trusts.

Corporate Interest Relief Generally

There is a limit to the Corporation Tax relief companies receive for interest and other finance costs. Most small company owners are unaffected, however, because the limit only applies to companies in international groups, or with associated companies overseas.

Furthermore, all groups can deduct up to £2 million per year of net interest expenses in the UK without restriction. Above this threshold, interest deductions are generally capped at a maximum of 30% of taxable earnings in the UK before interest, taxes, depreciation and amortisation (EBITDA).

We will take a closer look at the pros and cons of using a company to invest in residential property in Chapter 24.

More Information on Interest and Finance Costs

For more information on which interest and finance costs are eligible for tax relief if you are a landlord, see the Taxcafe.co.uk guide *'How to Save Property Tax'*.

It is important to understand that the interest relief restriction does not alter which interest and finance costs may be claimed by a landlord: it only alters the rate of tax relief available.

Chapter 4

The Timetable

Fortunately, the withdrawal of tax relief on mortgage interest for residential landlords has been rolled out gradually.

Last year (2019/20) 25% of your mortgage interest was still fully tax deductible. The remaining 75% qualifies for the 20% basic-rate tax reduction only.

This year (the 2020/21 tax year, which started on 6th April 2020) you are not able to claim any interest as a tax deductible expense, just the 20% tax reduction.

The timetable has been as follows:

- 2017/18   75% deducted as normal, 25% as basic-rate reduction
- 2018/19   50% deducted as normal, 50% as basic-rate reduction
- 2019/20   25% deducted as normal, 75% as basic-rate reduction
- 2020/21   All finance costs relieved at basic-rate only

Example
Oz has self-employment income just in excess of the higher-rate tax threshold each year. He also receives rental profits of £20,000 before deducting his interest costs, which amount to £6,000 each year. Oz pays tax as follows on his rental income:

	2016/17	2017/18	2018/19	2019/20	2020/21
Profit before interest	20,000	20,000	20,000	20,000	20,000
Less: Interest	6,000	4,500	3,000	1,500	0
	(100%)	(75%)	(50%)	(25%)	Nil
Taxable profit	14,000	15,500	17,000	18,500	20,000
Tax @ 40% (A)	5,600	6,200	6,800	7,400	8,000
Basic rate relief on	0	1,500	3,000	4,500	6,000
Equals: (B)	0	300	600	900	1,200
Tax payable (A-B)	£5,600	£5,900	£6,200	£6,500	£6,800

As we can see, the tax Oz pays on his rental income has increased from £5,600 to £6,800 – an increase of £1,200.

In Chapter 1, we mentioned that some landlords who are higher-rate taxpayers can make a rough and ready estimate of how much extra tax they're paying because of the interest relief restriction by simply multiplying their interest costs by 20%.

This holds true in Oz's case – his total interest costs are £6,000 and multiplying by 20% we get £1,200.

As stated previously, however, this rough and ready estimate cannot be relied on by all taxpayers.

This Year May Be Different

Although the mortgage tax relief restriction is now in full force, this year things may be very different for some landlords. Those who have experienced a significant drop in income may be completely unaffected by the mortgage tax change.

Example revised
Let's say the income Oz receives from self-employment falls from just over £50,000 last year (the higher-rate threshold) to £35,000 this year. Let's also assume his taxable rental profit (before deducting interest payments) falls from £20,000 to £15,000. Oz will now have total taxable income of £50,000 and will be a basic-rate taxpayer.

This means he will be completely unaffected by the mortgage tax relief restriction this year. He will receive a tax reduction equal to 20% of his interest payments – but he would have only enjoyed 20% tax relief if his interest was still a fully deductible expense.

This is probably little consolation to Oz because he has suffered a severe drop in his after-tax income. After paying income tax and national insurance on his self-employment income and income tax on his rental income, he will be left with an after-tax disposable income of £35,246.

If his income had stayed the same, he would have ended up with after-tax disposable income of just over £45,896, even with tax relief on his interest restricted.

In this example Oz is not affected by the mortgage tax relief restriction at all this year but is nevertheless £10,000 worse off overall because his income has fallen so sharply.

Some landlords will have seen their income fall this year, but will still be affected by the mortgage tax relief restriction. This will be the case if their taxable income has fallen but they are still higher-rate taxpayers, i.e. if their taxable income is still over £50,000 (£43,430 for Scottish taxpayers).

Preparing for the Change

Some landlords are still unaware of the full significance of the mortgage tax change.

This is because, at the time of writing, most have only recently paid their tax bills for the 2018/19 tax year – when just one half of their interest was denied full tax relief. So landlords have not felt all of the pain in their wallets or purses yet.

Others have been preparing for the change since it was announced in 2015, with some taking fairly drastic action, including transferring existing properties into a limited company.

If you believe what journalists say some landlords have even sold up and exited the business altogether. We suspect this will have happened for other reasons as well, including the insane amount of regulation landlords have to cope with these days and the stress sometimes caused by problem tenants.

It's important to point out that, even at this late stage, you should not panic and do something you will regret later.

We don't think many landlords are taking the 'nuclear option' and selling up completely. Most will simply take the tax hit on the chin. In recent times many landlords have enjoyed healthy rental profits thanks to low interest rates and may still be better off than they were a few years ago, despite the tax change. In some parts of the country landlords have also enjoyed excellent capital growth and may decide that a higher Income Tax bill is worth paying in return for less heavily taxed capital gains.

Tax Planning this Year (2020/21)

We've been publishing this guide for several years now and every year we advise readers what steps they can take to reduce the cost of the mortgage tax change.

However, the tax planning action landlords should take this year may be different to previous years.

The mortgage tax change increases your taxable income, which means you could end up with more income taxed at 40%, or even higher rates. However, with many landlords experiencing a significant drop in income this year, either from their property business, or from their main job or another business, it is possible many will find themselves in a *lower* tax bracket – even though this was expected to be the year when tax bills peak.

In this situation it may be worth postponing certain types of tax deductible spending until your income rises again and you find yourself in a higher tax bracket where more tax relief is available.

Another consequence of having less income is that many landlords will have smaller cash resources or may be unwilling to spend the cash they have. Saving tax often requires spending money!

Finally, note that although the mortgage tax change has now been fully phased in, it is not too late to do some of the long-term tax planning we discuss in later chapters, such as transferring properties to your spouse or partner (Chapter 23) or transferring properties into a company (Chapters 24 to 27).

The mortgage tax change is probably here to stay, at least for the foreseeable future, so any tax planning action you take could reap rewards for years to come.

Chapter 5

The 20% Tax Reduction: How it Works

Although interest costs are no longer a tax deductible expense for residential landlords, you can still claim a 20% 'tax reduction'.

So, if you have £10,000 of mortgage interest your Income Tax bill will be reduced by £2,000 (£10,000 x 20%).

The tax reduction is not always calculated as 20% of your finance costs. There are some restrictions to prevent landlords receiving too much relief.

The tax reduction is calculated as 20% of the *lowest* of:

- Your dwelling-related finance costs not allowed as a deduction

- The profits of the property business, after deducting any brought forward property losses

- Your 'adjusted total income' (total taxable income less savings income, dividends and your personal allowance)

Looking at the first bullet point, this number is 25% of your finance costs in 2017/18, 50% in 2018/19, 75% in 2019/20 and 100% this year (2020/21).

The second bullet point could apply if you have unusually low rental profits, for example if your properties have lain empty for longer than usual or you have unusually high repair costs. It may also apply if there are significant losses brought forward from previous tax years.

The third bullet point may apply if you have a relatively low level of income overall.

If bullet points two or three apply and restrict the tax reduction, the excess finance costs are carried forward to future tax years.

Example

In 2020/21 Latif has salary income of £40,000 and rental income of £20,000 from a student flat. He also has other property expenses of £3,000, so his taxable rental profit is £17,000. He pays £7,000 in mortgage interest but none of this is deducted when calculating his taxable rental profit.

*His tax reduction is calculated as 20% of the **lowest** of:*

- *His dwelling-related finance costs = £7,000*

- *His taxable rental profit = £17,000*

- *Adjusted total income (£40,000+£17,000–£12,500) = £44,500*

(The personal allowance for 2020/21 is £12,500)

In this example Latif can claim a tax reduction equal to 20% of his finance costs and is unaffected by the other restrictions.

Example revised

The facts are the same as before except we will assume Latif's taxable rental profit has fallen to just £5,000 because his student flat has lain empty for many months and he has incurred higher than expected repair costs. His tax reduction is calculated as 20% of the lowest *of:*

- *His dwelling-related finance costs = £7,000*

- *His taxable rental profit = £5,000*

- *Adjusted total income (£40,000+£5,000–£12,500) = £32,500*

In this example Latif can claim a tax reduction equal to 20% of his taxable rental profit: £5,000 x 20% = £1,000.

The excess finance costs (£2,000) will be carried forward to the next tax year and added to his finance costs for that year.

So if he also has £7,000 of finance costs in the next tax year his tax reduction will be 20% of £9,000 (unless his taxable rental profit or adjusted total income is lower than this).

Example revised again

The facts are the same as in the first example except Latif doesn't have any salary income, just rental income. His tax reduction is calculated as 20% of the lowest *of:*

- *His dwelling-related finance costs = £7,000*

- *His taxable rental profit = £17,000*

- *His adjusted total income (£17,000 – £12,500) = £4,500*

Latif can claim a tax reduction equal to 20% of his adjusted total income: £4,500 x 20% = £900. The excess finance costs (£2,500) can be carried forward to the next tax year.

Landlords with Losses

The 20% tax reduction may also be restricted if you have rental losses brought forward from previous tax years:

Example

During the previous 2019/20 tax year Ivana had a salary of £50,000 and gross rental income of £20,000. She paid £7,000 in mortgage interest and 25% of this (£1,750) was allowed as a tax deduction. She also had other property expenses of £3,000, so her taxable rental profit for the year was £15,250. She had rental losses of £19,000 brought forward from previous tax years, so her taxable rental profit was reduced to zero. The remaining loss of £3,750 is carried forward to 2020/21.

Her tax reduction for 2019/20 is calculated as 20% of the lowest *of:*

- *Her disallowed finance costs (£7,000-£1,750) = £5,250*

- *Her taxable rental profit = £0*

- *Adjusted total income (£50,000 + £0 – £12,500) = £37,500*

(£12,500 is the personal allowance for 2019/20 and 2020/21)

Ivana cannot claim a tax reduction for 2019/20 but the £5,250 of unrelieved interest is carried forward to the current 2020/21 tax year.

Example continued

During the current 2020/21 tax year Ivana once again has a salary of £50,000 and rental income of £20,000. She pays £7,000 in mortgage interest and none of this is allowed as a tax deduction. She has other property expenses of £2,500, so her taxable rental profit for the year is £17,500. She also has rental losses of £3,750 brought forward from the previous tax year, so her taxable rental profit is reduced to £13,750.

Her tax reduction for 2020/21 is calculated as 20% of the lowest of:

- *Finance costs not allowed (£7,000 + £5,250) = £12,250*

- *Her taxable rental profit = £13,750*

- *Adjusted total income (£50,000+£13,750–£12,500) = £51,250*

Ivana will receive a tax reduction equal to 20% of her £12,250 of unrelieved finance costs (£7,000 from this year and £5,250 from last year). Her tax bill will be reduced by £2,450 (£12,250 x 20%).

Summary

For the vast majority of landlords calculating the 20% tax reduction does not create any problems – they simply multiply their finance costs by 20%.

However, the tax reduction may be smaller if you have smaller than normal rental profits or rental losses from previous years.

You may have smaller than normal rental profits if your repair costs for the year are high or if your rental income has fallen. Many landlords will see their rental income fall this year as a result of the coronavirus crisis. In some cases it is possible their taxable rental profit will be smaller than their interest costs, which means the tax reduction will be smaller than normal.

The tax reduction may also be smaller if you have very low adjusted total income (e.g. if you have very little income from other sources and small rental profits).

If your tax reduction is restricted, the excess finance costs will be carried forward to future tax years.

Chapter 6

How Much Tax Will You Pay? Case Studies

In this chapter we'll look at how the mortgage tax change affects different property investors.

We'll look at how much tax different investors will pay, compared with what they would have paid if their mortgage interest was fully tax deductible.

This will help you understand the full impact of the mortgage tax change.

The higher-rate threshold is £50,000 this year and the personal allowance is £12,500. These numbers will be used throughout. Scottish taxpayers are subject to different tax rates (see further in Chapter 8).

Note, in the case studies that follow we use the term 'net rental income' which is rental income minus all tax deductible property expenses, except interest and other finance costs.

Case Study 1 – No Impact

Pearl is a retired widow who receives a pension of £20,000 per year and net rental income (before deducting her finance costs) of £18,000. She pays £6,000 interest on her buy-to-let mortgages, so her 'true' rental profit is £12,000.

Assuming there was no restriction to her mortgage interest tax relief, her total taxable income would be £32,000. The first £12,500 would be tax free and the rest would be taxed at 20% producing a tax bill of £3,900.

But with none of her interest allowed as a tax deductible expense her taxable income will be £38,000, resulting in a tax bill of £5,100. However, she will also be entitled to a tax reduction equal to 20% of her mortgage interest (£1,200), so her final tax bill will still be £3,900.

Comment – Pearl is completely unaffected by the tax change because her total taxable income remains below the £50,000 higher-rate threshold, i.e. none of her income ends up being taxed at 40%.

Those who will find themselves in a similar position include taxpayers who have relatively small amounts of income from other sources and small property portfolios, e.g. many retirees and non-working spouses.

Case Study 2
From 20% Tax to 40% Tax

Dave is a full-time landlord with rental income of £75,000. He pays £25,000 interest on his buy-to-let mortgages and has other property related expenses of £10,000, resulting in a true rental profit of £40,000.

Assuming no restriction to his mortgage interest relief, his total taxable income would be £40,000. The first £12,500 would be tax free and the rest would be taxed at 20%, producing a tax bill of £5,500.

But with none of his interest allowed as a tax deduction his taxable income will be £65,000. £15,000 will now be subject to higher-rate tax at 40%. He'll also be entitled to a tax reduction equal to 20% of his interest. His final tax bill will be £8,500.

Comment – Dave's tax bill is £3,000 higher thanks to the change. Because he cannot deduct his mortgage interest his taxable income increases by £25,000 and he becomes a higher-rate taxpayer. As a result he pays an additional 20% tax on £15,000 of his rental income.

This case study reveals that some landlords who would otherwise be basic-rate taxpayers will become higher-rate taxpayers thanks to the mortgage tax relief restriction.

You can perform a rough-and-ready 'back of the envelope' calculation to see if you will be affected in a similar way. First, estimate your taxable rental profit by taking your gross rental income and deducting an estimate of your property expenses (repairs, letting agent fees etc but NOT mortgage interest). Then add this to your other taxable income (salary, dividends, etc). If the total exceeds the higher-rate threshold (£50,000 in 2020/21) you are likely to end up with a higher tax bill.

Case Study 3
An Extra Tax Sting – Loss of Child Benefit

If Dave is also a parent and his family receives child benefit he could face an extra tax sting: the High Income Child Benefit Charge.

This kicks in when the highest earner in the household has taxable income over £50,000. Once your taxable income reaches £60,000 all of the family's child benefit is effectively lost thanks to the tax charge.

Because his mortgage interest is no longer a tax deductible expense Dave's taxable income increases from £40,000 to £65,000, so he goes from paying no child benefit tax charge to having all the family's child benefit effectively taken away.

How much extra tax will Dave pay? Based on current child benefit rates, Dave could end up paying anywhere from £1,095 (one child) to £3,271 (four children) or even more (£725 extra for each further qualifying child) in additional tax – on top of the £3,000 extra tax he pays by becoming a higher-rate taxpayer.

***Comment** – Many landlords will find themselves in a similar position, i.e. with taxable income over £50,000 now that their interest is no longer tax deductible. In some cases having to pay the child benefit charge will more than double the amount of extra tax you have to pay.*

Case Study 4
Higher-Rate Taxpayer – Best Case Scenario

Maureen is a landlord who also works full time. She earns a salary of £60,000 and net rental income of £40,000 (before deducting her finance costs). She pays £12,000 interest on her buy-to-let mortgages so her true rental profit is £28,000.

First let's calculate how much tax she would pay if there was no restriction to her mortgage interest tax relief. Because her salary already takes her over the £50,000 higher-rate threshold, she would pay 40% tax on her entire rental profit – £11,200.

However, with none of her interest allowed as a tax deductible expense she will have an additional £12,000 taxed at 40%, increasing her tax bill by £4,800. She will also be entitled to a tax reduction equal to 20% of her mortgage interest (£2,400), so her total tax bill will increase by £2,400.

Comment – *This is the best case scenario for a higher-rate taxpayer: her tax bill increases by an amount equivalent to 20% of her finance costs (because she's getting 20% tax relief instead of 40% tax relief). However, she doesn't get pushed into a higher tax bracket.*

Case Study 5
Personal Allowance Taken Away

Colleen is a landlord who also works full time. She earns a salary of £60,000 and net rental income of £65,000 (before deducting her finance costs). She pays £25,000 interest on her buy-to-let mortgages so her true rental profit is £40,000.

First we calculate how much tax she would pay if there was no restriction to her mortgage interest tax relief. With taxable income of £100,000 she would pay £27,500 in tax. The first £12,500 would be tax free; the next £37,500 would be taxed at 20% and the final £50,000 at 40%. (This includes the tax on her salary collected under PAYE.)

However, with none of her interest allowed as a tax deductible expense she will have taxable income of £125,000 and her personal allowance will be completely withdrawn.

(Your personal allowance is gradually withdrawn when your taxable income exceeds £100,000. For every additional £2 you earn you lose £1 of allowance. So with a personal allowance of £12,500 someone with taxable income of £125,000 or more will lose their whole personal allowance.)

Tax on income of £125,000 comes to £42,500. However, Colleen will also be entitled to a tax reduction equal to 20% of her mortgage interest (£5,000), so her final tax bill will be £37,500 – an increase of £10,000!

Comment – *Colleen suffers a double tax whammy: She no longer gets 40% tax relief on her mortgage interest and loses her personal allowance. Each tax sting costs her an additional £5,000.*

Quite a few landlords could find themselves in a similar position, in particular those with large but quite heavily geared property portfolios, i.e. those whose taxable rental 'profits' have increased sharply now their interest payments are no longer tax deductible.

Case Study 6
Existential Event – Income Drops by 50%

Katerina is a full-time landlord who owns a portfolio of residential rental properties producing net rental income of £125,000 per year. This is after deducting all the expenses of the business except her mortgage interest.

Her portfolio is heavily geared and her interest payments are £75,000 per year. Thus her true rental profit is £50,000 per year.

We'll assume Katerina has no other taxable income but does receive around £2,500 in child benefit and is the highest earner in her household.

Assuming there was no restriction to her mortgage tax relief, Katerina would have taxable income of £50,000 (if she had any more income she would be a higher-rate taxpayer). The first £12,500 would be tax free thanks to her personal allowance and the final £37,500 would be taxed at just 20% producing a total Income Tax bill of £7,500.

Furthermore, because her taxable income would not exceed £50,000 she would not have to pay the child benefit tax charge and would keep all of her £2,500 child benefit.

Her total after-tax disposable income would therefore be £45,000.

Now let's see how Katerina fares under the restriction to mortgage interest tax relief. Because her mortgage interest is no longer a tax deductible expense she will have a taxable rental profit of £125,000.

With this much taxable income she will lose all of her Income Tax personal allowance. Thus the first £37,500 will be taxed at 20% and the remaining £87,500 at 40% resulting in tax of £42,500.

Against this she will be able to claim a tax reduction of 20% of her mortgage interest (£15,000) leaving her with a total tax bill of £27,500.

She will also have to pay the full child benefit charge and will effectively lose roughly £2,500 of income, so her final after-tax disposable income will fall from £45,000 to £22,500:

£125,000 net rent - £75,000 interest - £27,500 tax = £22,500

Comment – *With her after-tax income falling by 50% it is unlikely that Katerina will be able to cover her household expenses and she will probably have to take drastic action to shore up her finances.*

This example illustrates that the main victims of the tax change are not "wealthier landlords with larger incomes", as the Government would have us believe. The main victims are landlords who have big buy-to-let portfolios but significant amounts of debt, i.e. those who earn significant amounts of rental income but have fairly modest rental profits.

These landlords are being forced to pay tax at 40% (and possibly 45%) on profits that do not exist and may face other tax penalties such as the loss of their Income Tax personal allowance and child benefit.

Case Study 7
Landlord with Dividend Income

Sinead is a landlord who also owns a graphic design company. She takes a salary of £12,500 out of her company and dividends of £40,000.

She also earns net rental income of £35,500 before deducting her interest costs. She pays £12,000 interest on her buy-to-let mortgages, so her true rental profit is £23,500.

With her mortgage interest no longer tax deductible, her taxable rental profit will be £35,500. Along with her salary of £12,500 this will take her taxable income up to £48,000.

Because this is still below the £50,000 higher-rate threshold all her taxable rental profit will be taxed at 20%, with an offsetting tax reduction of 20% on her mortgage interest. So at first glance it looks like she is unaffected by the mortgage tax change.

Where Sinead will feel the sting, however, is on her dividend income. Dividends are always treated as the top slice of income.

The first £2,000 of her dividend income will be tax free thanks to the dividend allowance and this will take her taxable income up to the £50,000 higher-rate threshold.

All of her remaining dividend income will be taxed at the 32.5% higher rate.

Because her taxable rental 'profits' have increased by £12,000 (the amount of her mortgage interest), £12,000 of her dividend income gets pushed over the higher-rate threshold where it is taxed at 32.5% instead of 7.5% – an increase of 25%.

Thus her final tax bill will increase by £3,000 (£12,000 x 25%).

Comment – *Many company owners will find themselves in a similar position. The July 2015 Budget contained two major tax bombshells for company owners who have separate property businesses:*

- *Dividend tax rates were increased by 7.5%*
- *The mortgage tax relief restriction was announced*

As we know from previous chapters, many landlords who are higher-rate taxpayers will see their tax bills increase by an amount equivalent to 20% of their mortgage interest.

However, for many company owners with dividend income the tax hit is 25%. For example, a company owner with £20,000 of buy-to-let interest could end up paying £5,000 more tax.

Case Study 8
Company Owner Denied Tax Reduction

Louise receives dividends of £50,000 from her family's pub company, although she does not work there. She also owns a flat from which she receives net rental income of £12,000 (before deducting her finance costs). She pays £7,000 interest, so her true rental profit is £5,000.

With none of her mortgage interest allowed as a tax deduction her taxable rental profit increases by £7,000 to £12,000. All of her rental profit is still tax free as it is covered by her £12,500 personal allowance. However, an additional £7,000 of her dividend income (that would have been covered by her personal allowance) will be taxed at 32.5% instead of 0% – a tax increase of £2,275.

And what about her 20% tax reduction? Remember from Chapter 5 this is calculated as 20% of the *lowest* of:

- Finance costs not allowed = £7,000

- Taxable rental profit = £12,000

- Adjusted total income (£12,000 – £12,500) = £0

Her dividends are not included in her adjusted total income so when we subtract her personal allowance from her taxable rental profit, her adjusted total income is reduced to zero (it cannot be reduced below zero).

Thus Louise cannot claim any tax reduction!

***Comment** – For someone who earns a modest rental profit of £5,000 a tax increase of £2,275 is pretty significant.*

Taxpayers who could find themselves in a similar position include silent shareholders who do not receive any salary income and have relatively small amounts of income from property.

Case Study 9
Additional Rate Tax

Ranjit, a full time landlord, receives net rental income of £200,000 after deducting all expenses except interest. His total allowable interest amounts to £75,000, giving him a true rental profit of £125,000.

Assuming no restriction to his mortgage interest, his total taxable income would be £125,000. The first £37,500 would be taxed at 20% and the rest at 40%, giving him a tax bill of £42,500.

However, with none of his interest allowed as a tax deduction, Ranjit's taxable income is increased to £200,000. The first £37,500 will be taxed at 20%, the next £112,500 at 40%, and the final £50,000 at the additional rate of 45%.

This gives Ranjit a total tax liability of £75,000, but he remains entitled to a tax reduction equal to 20% of his interest, i.e. £15,000. His final tax bill will therefore be £60,000.

Ranjit suffers an overall tax increase of £17,500. This represents an additional charge of 20% on the first £25,000 of his mortgage interest (taking him up to the additional rate tax threshold of £150,000) plus 25% on the remaining £50,000.

Comment – *Once the landlord's total taxable income exceeds the additional rate tax threshold of £150,000, the impact of the change in interest relief increases from 20% to 25%.*

This will affect many landlords with large residential property portfolios.

Don't Forget Payments on Account

The reduction in mortgage tax relief has resulted in many landlords having to make larger payments on account.

Payments on account are usually made twice a year and allow HMRC to collect some of the tax you owe early.

Although payments on account are not extra tax, they do affect your cashflow.

Many landlords will have felt the first effects of the mortgage tax change in January 2019 when their tax bills for 2017/18 fell due.

Some landlords will have seen their six monthly tax bills increase ever since, and these tax increases could continue into 2022.

Each payment on account is usually equal to half the *previous* year's self assessment tax.

Example
Remember Katerina from case study 6 above. In 2016/17 (before the tax change) her tax bill was £9,200.

Thus by 31ˢᵗ January 2018, she should have made a payment on account of £4,600 (£9,200/2) towards her 2017/18 tax bill. She will also have made another payment of £4,600 by 31ˢᵗ July 2018.

However, her actual tax bill for 2017/18 was £14,950, so a final balancing payment of £5,750 (£14,950 - £9,200) will have had to be made by 31ˢᵗ January 2019. At the same time she will also have made a payment on account of £7,475 (£14,950/2) towards her 2018/19 tax bill. Another payment of £7,475 was due by 31ˢᵗJuly 2019.

Her actual tax bill for 2018/19 was £18,360, so a final balancing payment of £3,410 (£18,360 - £14,950) had to be made by 31ˢᵗ January 2020. She also had to make a payment on account towards the next year's tax bill, and this time it was £9,180 (£18,360/2).

Another payment of £9,180 towards her 2019/20 tax bill would normally be due by 31ˢᵗ July 2020. However, to help people struggling with the coronavirus situation, the Government has allowed these payments to be deferred until 31ˢᵗ January 2021.

In summary, the total amount of tax payable by Katerina is set out below. The figures in brackets indicate the amounts she would have had to pay if the mortgage tax change had not been introduced.

31st January 2018	£4,397	(£4,397)
31st July 2018	£4,600	(£4,600)
31st January 2019	£13,225	(£3,850)
31st July 2019	£7,475	(£4,350)
31st January 2020	£12,590	(£3,840)
31st July 2020*	£0	(£0)
31st January 2021	£24,570	(£7,070)
31st July 2021	£11,250	(£3,750)
31st January 2022	£22,500	(£3,750)
31st July 2022	£15,000	(£3,750)

* Postponed until 31 January 2021

Assuming Katerina has taken up the Government's offer to postpone her July 2020 payment on account, she has £24,570 to pay by 31st January 2021.

This payment will be made up of:

- Her postponed July 2020 payment on account - £9,180
- Her balancing payment due for 2019/20 - £4,140
- Her first payment on account due for 2020/21 - £11,250

These figures assume her net rental income and interest payments remain unchanged throughout.

This is a key planning point. If Katerina's rental income has fallen this year because of the coronavirus situation, she may be able to apply to reduce her payments on account when she submits her 2019/20 tax return.

In other words, if she expects the taxable rental profit she earns between 6th April 2020 and 5th April 2021 to be lower than the previous year, she can apply to reduce the tax payments due by 31st January 2021 and 31st July 2021.

We'll look at payments on account again in the next chapter.

Chapter 7

How Much Will You Pay this Year (2020/21)?

In the previous chapter we looked at how much tax different landlords will pay, compared with what they would be paying if their mortgage interest was fully tax deductible.

In this chapter we'll look at how much tax different landlords are likely to pay this year (2020/21) compared with last year (2019/20) when *one quarter* of their interest was still tax deductible.

Higher-rate taxpayers can make a very rough estimate of how much extra tax they'll pay this year compared with last year by multiplying their interest costs by 5%.

So if your total interest costs are £20,000 your tax bill will be £1,000 higher this year compared with last year – *if you are looking at the mortgage tax relief restriction in isolation.*

However, this year some property investors may end up paying **less tax** than last year. This is because, thanks to the coronavirus situation, many landlords will earn less income this year – either from their property business or their main job or other business. Less income means less tax.

If your taxable income has fallen this year but, despite this, still exceeds the £50,000 higher-rate threshold, you will still be impacted by the mortgage tax change.

If your total taxable income is less than £50,000 this year, you will be completely unaffected by the mortgage tax change... but you could be worse off overall if your income has fallen.

Some landlords, as we shall see, will be completely unaffected by both the coronavirus situation and the mortgage tax change, some will be affected by both.

In the case studies that follow we once again use the term 'net rental income' which is rental income minus all tax deductible property expenses, except interest and other finance costs.

Note, income tax rates in 2019/20 and 2020/21 are the same.

Case Study 1 – Basic-Rate Taxpayer:
Unaffected by the Tax Change & the Coronavirus

Ivanka earns net rental income of £30,000 from some flats. She has no other income and her interest costs are £10,000 per year. Her flats have remained fully occupied and her tenants have paid all their rent.

Last year (2019/20) her income tax bill was £1,500, this year (2020/21) her tax bill is also £1,500. Ivanka is completely unaffected by the mortgage tax change because she is a basic-rate taxpayer. She is also completely unaffected by the coronavirus downturn because her rental income has not fallen.

Case Study 2 – Basic-Rate Taxpayer:
Unaffected by Tax Change, Affected by Coronavirus

Marla also normally earns net rental income of £30,000 from some flats and has no other income. Her interest costs are £10,000 per year. This year her net rental income has fallen to £25,000.

Last year (2019/20) her income tax bill was £1,500, this year (2020/21) her tax bill is just £500. Marla is completely unaffected by the mortgage tax change because she is a basic-rate taxpayer but her after-tax disposable income has fallen from £18,500 to £14,500 due to the coronavirus downturn.

Case Study 3: Higher-Rate Taxpayer:
Affected by the Tax Change, Unaffected by Coronavirus

Melania normally earns a salary and net rental income of £60,000 in total and pays £18,000 buy-to-let mortgage interest. She has continued to receive her full salary this year and her property business has been unaffected by the coronavirus situation.

Last year (2019/20) one quarter of her interest (£4,500) was tax deductible so her taxable income was £55,500. Her Income Tax bill was £9,700 less a £2,700 tax reduction (£13,500 x 20%) – £7,000 in total.

This year (2020/21) none of her interest is tax deductible so her taxable income will be £60,000. Her Income Tax bill will be £11,500 less a £3,600 tax reduction (£18,000 x 20%) – £7,900 in total.

Her Income Tax bill will increase by £900 – this is 5% of her mortgage interest, as per the rule of thumb outlined above.

If Melania has children she may also end up losing the final 45% of her child benefit if she is the highest earner in her household. If she has two children the additional child benefit charge will be £819 this year. Before the mortgage tax change was introduced she would have retained all of her child benefit.

Case Study 4: Older Higher-Rate Taxpayer: Affected by Tax Change and Coronavirus

Malia is over state pension age and hence not subject to National Insurance. She normally has combined pension, self-employment, and net rental income of £120,000 in total. Her buy-to-let mortgage interest comes to £15,000 per year. This year her combined pension, self-employment, and net rental income have fallen to £80,000 in total.

Last year (2019/20) one quarter of her interest (£3,750) was tax deductible so her taxable income was £116,250. Her Income Tax bill was £37,250 less a £2,250 tax reduction (three quarters of her interest £11,250 x 20%) – £35,000 in total.

This year (2020/21) none of her interest is tax deductible so her taxable income will be £80,000. Her tax bill will be £19,500 less a £3,000 tax reduction (£15,000 x 20%) – £16,500 in total.

Malia's after-tax disposable income has fallen from £70,000 last year to £48,500 this year. She is fully impacted by both the coronavirus downturn and the mortgage tax change. If her mortgage interest was fully tax deductible, she would have an extra £3,000 in her pocket (£15,000 mortgage interest x 20%).

44

Case Study 5: Younger Higher-Rate Taxpayer: Affected by Tax Change and Coronavirus

Malia's younger sister, Cassandra, also normally has combined pension, self-employment, and net rental income of £120,000 in total; also has buy-to-let mortgage interest of £15,000 per year; and has also suffered a reduction in her total combined pension, self-employment, and net rental income to £80,000 this year (2020/21).

In other words, her income and expenses are exactly the same as Malia, but she differs in one important respect: she is under state pension age and hence subject to National Insurance on her self-employment income.

Cassandra's self-employment income amounts to £60,000 in 2019/20 and £40,000 in 2020/21. This gives her National Insurance liabilities of £4,079 and £2,904 respectively, in addition to her Income Tax bills, which will be exactly the same as Malia's.

Hence, Cassandra's after-tax disposable income falls from £65,921 last year to £45,596 this year, as a result of both the mortgage tax change and the coronavirus crisis. Like Malia, she loses £3,000 of disposable income in 2020/21 because of the restriction in mortgage interest tax relief (£15,000 x 20% = £3,000).

Case Study 6: Higher-Rate Taxpayer: Unaffected by Tax Change, Affected by Coronavirus

Anton is a company owner who normally earns a combined salary and net rental income of £40,000 and gets his company to pay him a dividend of £40,000. He pays £10,000 in buy-to-let mortgage interest.

Last year (2019/20) one quarter of his interest (£2,500) was tax deductible so his taxable income was £77,500. The Income Tax payable was £14,725 less a £1,500 tax reduction for disallowed interest – £13,225 in total.

This year (2020/21) his rental income has fallen and his combined salary and net rental income is just £30,000. His company is also experiencing difficulty so he decides to halve the amount of dividend income he pays himself to £20,000. This is to protect his company's cash and avoid paying income tax at the 32.5% higher rate.

None of his interest is tax deductible this year so his taxable income is £50,000. The Income Tax payable is £4,850 less a £2,000 tax reduction for disallowed interest – £2,850 in total.

With taxable income of £50,000, Anton is a basic-rate taxpayer this year. This means he is completely unaffected by the mortgage tax change. However, this will probably be of little consolation because his after-tax disposable income has fallen from £56,775 to £37,150.

(We have assumed Anton's salary does not exceed the primary threshold, so he does not suffer any Class 1 National Insurance.)

Summary

Clearly there are lots of different permutations – every landlord is different. Some will be completely unaffected by both the mortgage tax change and the coronavirus crisis. Some will be affected by both.

The coronavirus situation will probably have a much bigger impact on most landlords' income this year than the mortgage tax change, especially where landlords have income from other sources (for example, another job or business) and those other incomes have been badly affected by the coronavirus.

Don't Forget Payments on Account

Some property investors face having to make much bigger payments on account because of the mortgage tax change.

For example, in the previous chapter we saw how Katerina's total tax payment due by the end of January 2021 will be £24,570. Admittedly, £9,180 of this is due to taking up the Government's offer to postpone her July 2020 payment on account but, even without this, she would still have had £15,390 to pay, compared with just £4,397 a few years previously.

But what if Katerina's rental income has fallen this year because of the coronavirus situation? In this case she may be able to apply to *reduce* her payments on account when she submits her 2019/20 tax return.

In other words, if she expects the taxable rental profit she will make between 6th April 2020 and 5th April 2021 to be lower than the previous year, she may be able to reduce the tax payments she has to make by 31st January 2021 and 31st July 2021.

For example, let's say Katerina expects her net rental income to fall from £125,000 to £100,000 this year. Her income tax bill would have been £30,000 but will now be just £15,000 (both figures include the child benefit charge).

However, the payments on account she would normally be making in January and July 2021 would be based on her tax bill for the *previous* 2019/20 tax year, which came to £22,500. That tax year ended on 5th April 2020, just after the lockdown was enforced, so most taxpayers' incomes were largely unaffected by the coronavirus situation in 2019/20.

Normally, Katerina would have to make a payment on account of £11,250 (£22,500/2) by 31st January 2021 and another payment of £11,250 by 31st July 2021.

However, because her income has fallen, she can apply to have the two payments on account reduced to £7,500 each (£15,000)/2). This means she gets to keep hold of an extra £3,750 in January 2021 and an extra £3,750 in July 2021.

Where your self-assessment liability for the current tax year can reasonably be expected to be less than that for the previous year, you can apply to reduce your payments on account to the appropriate level (i.e. half of your anticipated liability for the current year). You can do this when you submit your 2019/20 tax return.

You have to be careful when doing this, however. If you claim a reduction in your payments on account and then find you have more tax to pay than you expected, you will have to pay interest on the underpayment and potentially also a penalty if HMRC deem you to have acted negligently (although this is rare and will generally only apply if you have significantly underestimated your tax bill).

Taxpayers who think their income will be significantly lower this year should try to estimate their total taxable income as accurately as possible before they submit their 2019/20 tax returns.

This way you can compare your actual 2019/20 tax bill with your estimated 2020/21 tax bill. If the 2020/21 tax bill is significantly lower you should consider applying to reduce your payments on account.

Remember it's not just falling property income that will affect your payments on account. If you normally receive a salary, income from self employment, or company dividends, and any of this income has fallen this year, this may also provide grounds for reducing your payments on account.

Chapter 8

Scottish Landlords

The Scottish Parliament has power over Income Tax rates and thresholds applying to most forms of income received by Scottish taxpayers, including rental income.

However, the Scottish Parliament has no power over:

- Income Tax rates on dividends and savings income
- Personal allowances (and their withdrawal where income exceeds £100,000)
- The High Income Child Benefit Charge
- National Insurance
- Corporation Tax
- Capital Gains Tax
- The 'tax base' – i.e. the way in which a person's total taxable income is calculated

In most cases, an individual will be a Scottish taxpayer if they are a UK resident whose main home is in Scotland.

Individuals who are not Scottish taxpayers will continue to pay UK Income Tax rates on all their taxable income: including any rental profits on Scottish properties.

Implications for Scottish Landlords

Scottish landlords are subject to the restrictions on interest relief discussed throughout this guide. Their taxable rental profits will be calculated in exactly the same way as anyone else: but the rate of tax payable on those profits is different.

Scottish landlords receive the same 20% tax reduction for their interest costs as everyone else.

Scottish taxpayers who use a company to invest in property pay the same rate of Corporation Tax in their company as everyone else and also pay the same rates of tax on any dividends they receive.

Scottish landlords continue to pay Capital Gains Tax on any property sales (or transfers) at exactly the same rates as all other UK resident taxpayers.

Scottish Income Tax 2020/21

The following Income Tax rates apply for 2020/21:

£0 - £12,500	0%	Personal allowance (PA)
£12,500 - £14,585	19%	Starter rate
£14,585 - £25,158	20%	Basic rate
£25,158 - £43,430	21%	Intermediate rate
£43,430 - £100,000	41%	Higher rate
£100,000 - £125,000	61.5%	PA withdrawal
£125,000 - £150,000	41%	Higher rate
£150,000 +	46%	Top rate

Many Scottish taxpayers now pay more tax than those in the rest of the UK. For example, someone earning £50,000 in Scotland will pay £1,542 more tax this year than someone living elsewhere in the UK; someone earning £100,000 will pay £2,042 more tax.

The key number is £27,243. Those who earn more than £27,243 will pay more tax this year than those living elsewhere in the UK.

To date, Income Tax increases in Scotland have been relatively timid because the Scottish Government is worried about chasing away high earners. We strongly suspect that the 46% top rate will be increased again at some point in the future.

The key point to remember is that, like everyone else, a Scottish taxpayer's 'taxable income' from 2020/21 onwards is calculated before deducting **any** of their interest and finance costs on residential lettings.

Example

Robert lives in Scotland, earns a salary of £60,000, has net rental income (before finance costs) of £40,000, and pays £20,000 interest on his mortgages.

None of his interest is tax deductible so his taxable income is £100,000. The Income Tax payable will be £29,542 less a £4,000 tax reduction for disallowed interest – £25,542 in total (including amounts paid under PAYE on his salary).

If he lived anywhere else in the UK, his total Income Tax bill would be £23,500. So he pays £2,042 more tax because he lives in Scotland.

It is interesting to note that if he lived elsewhere in the UK <u>and</u> we assume there was no restriction in interest tax relief, his Income Tax bill would be just £19,500.

So his tax bill is £6,042 higher than it would have been "in the good old days" before both Scottish tax and the mortgage tax change were introduced.

As we can see, the tax increases applying to Scottish taxpayers have effectively compounded the effects of the dreadful restrictions placed on interest relief by the UK Government.

The higher tax rates applying to Scottish landlords also mean the amount of tax that might potentially be saved by pursuing the strategies outlined in this guide will be greater: making tax planning even more important for Scottish landlords.

Chapter 9

What if Interest Rates Change Significantly?

Thanks to the historically low level of interest rates, many landlords have been enjoying healthy rental profits for many years now.

Interest rates on buy-to-let mortgages have fallen further since the mortgage tax change was first announced in 2015. In some cases, falling interest rates will have more than compensated for the loss of tax relief on finance costs.

As a general rule of thumb, if your borrowing costs have fallen by 25%, you will be no worse off overall following the mortgage tax change.

This will be the case if you are a high-rate taxpayer and were previously enjoying exactly 40% tax relief on your borrowing costs, reduced to 20% from 2020/21 onwards.

Example

Joanne is a higher-rate taxpayer with a buy-to-let mortgage of £100,000. Before the mortgage tax change she was paying 4% interest – £4,000 per year. She enjoyed 40% tax relief (£1,600) so the net cost of her borrowing was £2,400.

She is currently paying 3% interest – £3,000 per year. She now only enjoys 20% tax relief (£600) but the net cost of her borrowing is still £2,400.

As we can see, Joanne's borrowing costs have fallen by 25% and this completely covers the loss of tax relief, meaning she is no worse off than before.

According to Moneyfacts, between February 2015 and February 2020 the average five-year fixed rate for buy-to-let mortgages fell from 4.39% to 3.20% – a drop of 27%.

Since then the Bank of England has cut interest rates twice because of the coronavirus crisis and many lenders have followed suit and lowered rates.

Of course not all landlords will have seen their borrowing costs fall so sharply.

Some lenders have reportedly increased rates since the onset of the coronavirus crisis to cover the risk of tenants defaulting on their rent payments. Some have apparently imposed stricter lending criteria, steering clear of properties that are more exposed to vulnerable sectors, such as holiday lets.

What if Interest Rates Increase?

It's impossible to predict what will happen to interest rates. There's a good chance they will stay very low for a very long time.

However, because property is a long-term investment it's probably a good idea to "stress test" your portfolio to see how you would cope with a big increase in interest rates, especially now that the tax relief on your mortgage interest has been reduced.

Example – Without the Tax Change
Campbell is a landlord and also earns a salary of £60,000. He owns a property which cost him £100,000 and has a £75,000 interest only mortgage costing 3% (i.e. £2,250 per year). He receives rental income of £6,000 per year and his other tax deductible expenses come to £1,000.

If his mortgage interest was fully tax deductible he would have a taxable rental profit of £2,750 and as a higher-rate taxpayer he would pay 40% tax (£1,100), leaving him with a total after-tax rental profit of £1,650.

Example – After the Tax Change
With his mortgage interest no longer tax deductible his taxable rental profit will now be £5,000 resulting in a tax liability of £2,000. However, he'll also be entitled to a tax reduction of £450 (£2,250 x 20%), reducing his overall tax bill on this property to £1,550. His after-tax rental profit has therefore fallen from £1,650 to £1,200.

Obviously Campbell is upset that he is paying more tax but he is still making a positive rental return on the property. However, let's see what happens if interest rates increase significantly in the future.

Example continued

The facts are exactly the same except Campbell ends up paying 5% interest in a future tax year (£3,750). His taxable rental profit will still be £5,000 resulting in a tax liability of £2,000. He'll also be entitled to a tax reduction of £750 (£3,750 x 20%), reducing his overall tax bill on the property to £1,250. However, his after-tax rental profit will now be £0:

Rental income	*£6,000*
Less:	
Interest	*£3,750*
Other costs	*£1,000*
Net tax	*£1,250*
After-tax profit	*£0*

Campbell is now receiving no return from the property on the income side and must rely purely on capital growth instead.

He may be prepared to accept this outcome if he thinks the property will continue to rise in value.

However, he won't have any rental income left over to build any sort of contingency fund to protect against any unexpected costs and to cover any periods when the property is empty.

He will have to rely on his other income to cover any unexpected property expenses – possibly acceptable for just one property but his finances could be placed in a precarious position if he owns many properties.

In this example we assumed that the interest rate on Campbell's mortgage increases from 3% to 5%. Although this would be a significant increase from current levels, interest rates have been far higher in the past. Just before the 2008 financial crisis, mortgage rates of 6-7% were not uncommon.

We also assumed that Campbell's rental income does not increase. Rent increases, where possible, can reduce much of the tax sting landlords now face, as we shall see in Chapter 11.

Summary

With mortgage interest rates at historically low levels many landlords will be able to absorb the higher tax bills resulting from the restriction in tax relief on their finance costs.

However, if interest rates were to increase significantly at some point in the future, some landlords, in particular those with high loan to value ratios, could see all their rental profits disappear due to higher interest and tax charges.

Chapter 10

How to Beat the Tax Increase

In the chapters that follow we'll take a look at some of the things landlords can do to reduce the impact of the tax change including:

- Increasing rent
- Tax deductible spending on properties
- Employing family members
- Making pension contributions
- Paying off mortgages
- Selling properties
- Managing dividends (company owners)
- Emigrating
- Investing in other types of property
- Converting properties to a different use
- Using alternative investment structures
- Transferring properties to spouses
- Using a company

We suspect that many landlords will simply take the tax hit on the chin. Why? Because although they'll end up with less income than before, their properties will continue to produce positive rental profits thanks to the low level of interest rates.

Remember before interest rates were reduced following the 2008 financial crisis it wasn't uncommon for property investors to make rental *losses* year after year. They were happy to accept this outcome because their properties were rising in value and generating attractive capital gains.

Many property investors do not depend on their properties for income and invest primarily for capital growth. These landlords may be happy to accept a smaller after-tax rental income if their properties continue to rise in value.

Those that do depend on their properties for income may find that there is still no alternative investment that produces better returns.

However, this could all change if interest rates increase significantly at some point in the years ahead. If that happens more landlords may feel the need to sell up or take other action.

Those landlords who will feel the need to act soon are those who have large property portfolios and large amounts of debt. Remember Katerina from Case Study 6 in Chapter 6? She saw her after-tax income fall from £45,000 to £22,500. In Chapter 18 we'll take a look at whether she should sell some of her properties.

Chapter 11

Increasing Rent to Cover Tax Bills

In the days following the July 2015 Budget, press articles stated that many landlords were intending to increase the rent they charge to cover the mortgage tax increase. In other words, many landlords were intending to pass on the tax increase to their tenants.

In this chapter we'll show you how much extra rent you would have to charge to do this and whether this strategy is viable.

Example
Matt earns a salary of £60,000 and also receives rental income of £20,000. He pays £10,000 interest on his buy-to-let mortgages and we'll ignore his other property costs to keep the example simple.

In 2016/17, before the tax change, his interest was fully tax deductible so his taxable rental profit was £10,000. After paying 40% tax he was left with £6,000.

Now let's move forward to 2020/21 and assume Matt's rental income has increased to £23,333.

He'll pay 40% tax (£9,333) but will also be entitled to a tax reduction equal to 20% of his mortgage interest (£2,000). All in all Matt will be left with £6,000:

> *£23,333 rent - £10,000 interest - £7,333 net tax = £6,000*

Matt is no worse off following the tax change because the increase in his rental income covers the increase in his tax bill.

By how much does your rental income have to increase to cover the extra tax you will now pay? As a rule of thumb, if you're a higher-rate taxpayer, you can calculate the extra rent you will need by multiplying your interest bill by one third.

Matt in the above example pays £10,000 interest so he must increase his rental income by £3,333 (£10,000/3) to cover the extra tax he will pay. He'll pay 40% tax on this extra rent which will leave him with an additional £2,000 – exactly the amount of tax relief he loses on his mortgage interest.

This is very much a "back of the envelope" calculation and will not apply to all taxpayers. For example, those who also end up paying the child benefit charge or losing their personal allowance will have to charge even more rent.

Note too that, although Matt ends up with the same amount of rental income after tax, we have not taken account of inflation. Matt may need to charge even more rent to cover the general increases in his other property costs and his own cost of living.

Are Landlords Able to Increase their Rents?

Someone in the same position as Matt would have to increase the rent they charge by 16.67% to keep their after-tax rental income the same. The increases would have to be even greater than this to compensate for inflation as well.

It's worth noting that Matt's interest costs are probably quite high relative to his rental income. Landlords with lower interest costs do not have to increase their rents as much. For example, if Matt's interest costs were just £5,000 per year he would have to increase his rent by just 8.33% in total to cover his increased tax bill.

According to the Office for National Statistics, between January 2015 and April 2020, private rental prices in the UK increased by 9%. However, the ability to increase rent has varied from one part of the country to another and, of course, from property to property. Some landlords have been able to increase their rental income much more than others in recent years.

The coronavirus crisis has probably capped most landlords' ability to increase rents, at least in the short term. Apparently some landlords are now being forced to reduce rents to attract tenants.

In summary, it is by no means certain that landlords can cover their increased tax bills by simply increasing the rent they charge. However, some landlords in some parts of the country will probably have been able to claw back at least some of the extra tax they are paying by increasing rents.

Chapter 12

Postponing (or Accelerating) Tax Deductible Expenses

If you think you will end up in a higher tax bracket in a future tax year, it is possible to save tax by postponing certain types of spending on your properties.

For example, if you expect to be a basic-rate taxpayer this year but a higher-rate taxpayer in a future tax year, you can enjoy 40% tax relief instead of 20% tax relief on the spending you postpone.

For the current 2020/21 tax year, the key tax thresholds are:

- £50,000*   Higher-rate tax + Child benefit tax charge
- £100,000   Personal allowance withdrawal
- £150,000   Additional rate tax

  * £43,430 higher-rate threshold for Scottish taxpayers

In previous editions of this guide we pointed out that some property investors should consider postponing certain types of spending until the current 2020/21 tax year.

With none of your interest tax deductible this year, you could end up in a higher tax bracket and therefore enjoy more tax relief on your spending this year compared with previous years.

This year, as it turns out, may be another year when it pays to postpone certain types of tax deductible spending. Thanks to the coronavirus crisis, many landlords may find themselves in a *lower* tax bracket this year, even though none of their interest is tax deductible.

This may be the case if your rental income from your property business has fallen or if your income from other sources has fallen.

Maximising tax relief is just one consideration. Many landlords may wish to postpone non-essential spending on their properties to preserve their cash in these uncertain times.

Example

Ron is a full-time landlord who normally earns net rental income of £60,000. This is after deducting all his regular property expenses except his interest costs, which come to £15,000. He has no other income.

With none of his interest tax deductible Ron would normally be a higher-rate taxpayer this year (2020/21) and pay 40% tax on the final £10,000 of his income. This means he would normally enjoy 40% tax relief on up to £10,000 of spending on his properties.

However, this year things have turned out very differently and he expects his net rental income to fall to just below the £50,000 higher-rate threshold.

Ron had planned to spend £6,000 replacing the kitchen in one of his properties. But if he spends the money this year he will enjoy just 20% tax relief (£1,200). If he spends the money in a future tax year, when he is a higher-rate taxpayer again, he will enjoy 40% tax relief (£2,400). Ron can therefore save £1,200 by simply postponing his spending.

The problem for Ron is he cannot know for certain that he will be a higher-rate taxpayer next year. Perhaps his income will remain depressed for more than one year.

And there is only so much spending on properties that is truly discretionary and can be postponed. A new kitchen may make the property much easier to rent out if Ron is competing with lots of landlords in his area. In other words, it may be in Ron's interest to replace the kitchen this year, even if he enjoys much less tax relief.

We'll take a closer look at what types of spending it may be possible to postpone later in the chapter.

Example

Kathryn is a landlord who also has a significant amount of income from other sources. She would normally expect to have taxable income of around £100,000 this year. However, this year she expects her income to fall to around £75,000.

She will still be a higher-rate taxpayer this year and enjoy 40% tax relief on up to £25,000 of spending on her properties. However, because she has high outgoings (including school fees) she decides to limit the amount she spends on her properties this year to protect her cash.

Higher Rate Threshold Planning

You will only save tax by postponing tax deductible expenditure if your spending attracts more tax relief next year (or another future year) than this year.

Typically, tax savings will arise if both of these conditions are met:

i)   Your taxable income this year (2020/21) is already *below* the £50,000 higher-rate threshold. Or it will fall *below* the threshold if you spend the extra money this year. This means you will only enjoy basic-rate tax relief (20%) on some or all of your extra spending.

ii) If you spend the extra money next year (2021/22), your taxable income will NOT fall below the higher-rate threshold. Or, if it does, it will be to a lesser extent than if you spent the money this year. This means you will enjoy higher-rate tax relief (40%) on either all of your extra spending, or on more of it than this year.

Only some landlords will be able to save tax by postponing their spending. Most of those who expect to have taxable income well over the higher-rate threshold this year will not be able to save tax by postponing tax deductible expenditure.

For example, if you have taxable income of, say, £75,000 this year and £85,000 next year, you are unlikely to save tax by postponing expenses (because, unless the expenses exceed £25,000, you will enjoy higher-rate tax relief in either year in any case).

A problem with this type of tax planning is that most taxpayers simply do not know what their taxable income will be this year or next year, although if your income is relatively stable (as it usually is for many who earn salaries and rental income) it should be fairly easy to estimate.

A further complication is we do not know what the higher-rate threshold will be next year – essential for this type of tax planning. However, we do not expect the higher-rate threshold to be much different to what it is at present: £50,000. The Government previously announced that the higher-rate threshold will be increased with inflation, but this promise could be broken in these uncertain economic times.

The Other Key Tax Thresholds

The £50,000 Child Benefit Threshold

If you expect your taxable income to rise above £50,000 next year, there's another reason you may be able to save tax by postponing tax deductible spending on your properties.

If you're the highest earner in a household that receives child benefit you have to pay the High Income Child Benefit Charge once your income rises above £50,000.

Once your income reaches £60,000 you face the maximum charge and all the family's child benefit is effectively withdrawn.

If you end up in the £50,000-£60,000 tax bracket next year you could suffer an effective marginal Income Tax rate of 51% if you have one child (higher if you have more children).

So if you can postpone some of your 2020/21 spending until 2021/22, you may be able to reduce your taxable income and enjoy 51% or more tax relief!

Example
Let's say Ron from the above example is also the highest earner in a household which receives £1,820 child benefit for two children.

We know Ron expects to have a taxable rental profit of around £50,000 this year and £60,000 next year.

If Ron postpones replacing the kitchen until next year his taxable income will fall to £54,000 which means he will enjoy 40% tax relief and save £1,092 in child benefit. This brings the total tax saving he has achieved by postponing his expenditure up to £3,492, which is 58%.

Accelerating Spending

Some landlords, with income above the £60,000 threshold, may be able to avoid the Child Benefit Charge by doing the opposite – *accelerating* their tax deductible expenditure.

In other words, it may be better to spend money this year (2020/21) instead of next year (2021/22).

Example

Thelma is a landlord and the highest earner in a household which receives £2,545 child benefit for three children.

Let's say she normally has taxable income of £70,000 but expects this to fall to £63,000 this year because of the coronavirus crisis.

Let's say Thelma also plans to spend £8,000 on a replacement kitchen in one of her rental properties.

If she spends the money <u>this year</u> her taxable income will fall further to £55,000 which means she will recoup half her child benefit – £1,273. In total she will enjoy 56% tax relief on her spending.

If she spends the money <u>next year</u>, when her income has recovered, her taxable income will fall to £62,000 which means she will still lose all of her child benefit (because her taxable income will still be more than £60,000). In total she will enjoy just 40% tax relief on her spending

Spending more money when your income has fallen is somewhat counterintuitive and probably not for all landlords. Some will no doubt prefer to hold onto their precious cash until they feel more secure about the economic picture.

The £100,000 Threshold

If you expect your taxable income to rise above £100,000 next year, you may be able to save tax by postponing tax deductible spending on your properties until then.

This is because when your taxable income rises above £100,000 your personal allowance is gradually withdrawn. It's withdrawn at the rate of £1 for every £2 of income you have over £100,000.

We don't know what the personal allowance will be next year. The Government has promised to increase it in line with inflation but, with the public finances in such a precarious state, we don't know for sure if this will happen.

For the sake of simplicity we will assume that the personal allowance will be the same next year as this year: £12,500. This means that once your taxable income gets to £125,000 you will have no personal allowance left at all.

If you end up in the £100,000-£125,000 tax bracket in 2021/22 you will suffer an effective marginal Income Tax rate of 60%.

Thus if you can postpone some of your spending until then you may be able to reduce your taxable income and enjoy 60% tax relief.

Example
Magalie is a landlord who would normally expect to have total taxable income of around £120,000 this year. Because of the coronavirus crisis, however, she expects her income to fall temporarily below £100,000, even though none of her finance costs are tax deductible.

If she incurs an additional £20,000 of tax deductible expenditure this year she will enjoy just 40% tax relief. If she spends the money next year she will enjoy 60% tax relief – an additional tax saving of £4,000.

Of course, Magalie may not know for certain that her income will rise back to £120,000 next year. Perhaps her income will remain depressed for more than one year.

Accelerating Spending

Some landlords, with income above the £100,000 threshold this year may be able to enjoy 60% tax relief by doing the opposite – *accelerating* their tax deductible expenditure.

Example
Basil is a landlord who would normally expect to have total taxable income of around £150,000 this year. Because of the coronavirus crisis, however, he now expects his taxable income to fall to around £125,000 this year, even though none of his finance costs are tax deductible.

If he incurs an additional £10,000 of tax deductible expenditure this year he will claw back £5,000 of his personal allowance and enjoy 60% tax relief on the additional expenditure. If he spends the money next year he will not claw back any of his personal allowance and will thus enjoy just 40% tax relief. (This is assuming his income rises back to around £150,000 next year, something which is not guaranteed.)

As with Thelma in the earlier example, spending more money when your income has fallen is probably not for all landlords. Some will prefer to hold onto their cash for now.

The £150,000 Threshold

If your taxable income has fallen this year but you expect it to rise above £150,000 in a future year, you may be able to save tax by postponing tax deductible spending on your properties until then.

Once your income rises above £150,000 you become an additional rate taxpayer and pay Income Tax at 45%. You may be able to save tax by postponing spending on your properties but the savings may be quite modest. You will enjoy tax relief at 45% instead of 40% which isn't a huge difference.

What Spending Can be Postponed or Accelerated?

If you spend money on your properties, the expense is normally treated as either a repair or an improvement.

Repairs are immediately tax deductible and will save you Income Tax. Obvious examples of repairs are things that require urgent attention: broken windows, faulty boilers, etc. This type of repair is normally dealt with by the landlord immediately so discretionary tax planning doesn't come into the picture.

Improvements are not so good from a tax-saving perspective because tax relief is only provided when the property is sold and will only save you up to 28% Capital Gains Tax. Improvements are generally new features that were not present in the property before and therefore increase its value: extensions, attic conversions, etc.

Between these two extremes are repairs that provide full Income Tax relief AND may increase the value of your property and/or increase its rental potential.

Examples include: New kitchens, new bathrooms, double glazing, and most decorating costs. Many landlords think of these as improvements but often they are fully tax-deductible repairs... provided you follow the rules. To be treated as repairs, it is important that you replace old items with broadly equivalent new items and do not add something new that was not present before.

For example, replacing a tatty old kitchen is usually a tax-deductible repair. If you add extra kitchen units or sockets, these additional items will be improvements. Replacing a pea-green bathroom is a tax-deductible repair. Installing a shower or downstairs toilet where there wasn't one before is an improvement.

When replacing old items it is also important that you do not substantially upgrade the quality – that would be an improvement. However, it IS acceptable to install items that are of superior quality when they are simply the nearest modern equivalent, for example, replacing old single glazing with double glazing.

Although this is a tax-efficient way to spend your rental profits, there is no guarantee that this type of spending will always increase the value of your property or your rental income (or enough to make it worthwhile). There's also clearly a limit to the amount of this type of repair you can carry out, so it is not a permanent solution to your Income Tax problem.

See the Taxcafe.co.uk guide *'How to Save Property Tax'* for more details on which items qualify as tax deductible repairs.

Other Spending You May be Able to Postpone (or Accelerate)

To postpone, or accelerate, expenditure, there needs to be a degree of discretion over the timing. This will not always be the case: a broken window will usually need to be replaced immediately.

Other expenditure is related to a specific time period and will generally have to be claimed as an expense of that period, regardless of when you actually pay it. Examples include ground rent, insurance premiums and utility bills (where these are paid by the landlord). (The position on items of this nature will differ under the 'cash basis', so we will return to this point in Chapter 28.)

Nonetheless, there are some items that allow for a degree of discretion over the timing of your expenditure.

Replacements

Under 'replacement of domestic items relief' (formerly known as 'replacement furniture relief'), landlords can claim the cost of replacing movable items provided in fully or partly furnished residential properties: such as furniture, carpets, white goods and electrical equipment.

Such expenditure could often be postponed by a short period in order to obtain a better rate of tax relief. For example, you might be able to get a few extra months out of an old carpet: provided there are no safety issues involved!

There might even be a case for extending the life of faulty equipment, even if the overall pre-tax cost will be greater.

Example
Hermione is a basic-rate taxpayer this year (2020/21) but hopes her income will be higher next year and that she will be a higher-rate taxpayer. There is a faulty washing machine in one of her rental properties and it will inevitably need replacing in the near future. A replacement will cost £600 but a temporary repair costing £75 will keep the machine going into the 2021/22 tax year.

If Hermione replaces the machine in 2020/21, she will get tax relief at just 20%, giving her a net, after tax, cost of £480.

If she has the temporary repair carried out in 2020/21 and then replaces it in 2021/22, her total pre-tax expenditure will be more (£675), but her tax relief will amount to £15 in 2020/21 (£75 x 20%) and £240 in 2021/22 (£600 x 40%). Her total cost, after tax, is thus £420.

The saving in this example is not very much (just £60), but it does illustrate the fact that an overall saving can sometimes arise even when the total pre-tax cost is greater.

Car Sales and Equipment Purchases

Residential landlords are generally unable to claim capital allowances on furniture and equipment within their rental properties. They may, however, claim capital allowances on cars and other equipment purchased for their own use within their business.

Equipment, other than cars, which is purchased for business use, will generally attract immediate 100% tax relief under the annual investment allowance: although the relief claimed must be reduced to reflect any private use.

Cars used in the business generally only attract writing down allowances at either 6% or 18%, depending on the level of their CO2 emissions. These allowances must also be reduced to reflect private use of the vehicle.

When a car with business use is sold, however, there will generally be a balancing allowance (again reduced to reflect private use).

Hence, landlords facing an increase in their marginal tax rate can save tax by postponing the purchase of new equipment and/or the sale of a car used in their business.

Example
Harry's taxable income has fallen this year (2020/21) due to the coronavirus crisis. He expects it to increase from £100,000 this year to £120,000 in 2021/22, giving him a marginal tax rate of 60% (see above).

Harry wants to buy a new laptop for £1,000, which he will use 90% in his business. He also wants to replace his car, which is used 75% for business purposes.

Harry's car cost £35,000 in 2015 and is now worth just £10,000. By the end of 2019/20, he had claimed writing down allowances of £11,431 on the car (before the reduction to reflect private use), leaving £23,569 of unrelieved expenditure carried forward.

When Harry buys his new laptop, he will be able to claim £900 under the annual investment allowance (£1,000 x 90%).

When he sells his car, he will be able to claim a balancing allowance of £13,569 (£23,569 - £10,000), reduced to £10,177 to reflect private use.

Harry's total claim will come to £11,077 (£900 + £10,177) and, if he does all this in 2020/21, he'll save £4,431 in Income Tax (at 40%).

But, if Harry waits until 2021/22 to buy his laptop and sell his car, his saving will be £6,646 (at 60%), i.e. £2,215 more!

We have assumed Harry disclaims the writing down allowance on his old car in 2020/21, in order to maintain his balancing allowance at the same level on a sale in 2021/22. This will often be worth doing where a car is to be sold the following year and the taxpayer's marginal Income Tax rate is set to increase.

Harry has saved tax by postponing the sale of his old car to a year in which he has a higher marginal tax rate and this is what has produced most of his additional tax saving (£2,035 out of the total additional saving of £2,215).

He has also made a further additional saving of £180 by postponing the purchase of his new laptop.

However, it may not be worth postponing the purchase of a new car, even when the landlord's marginal Income Tax rate is expected to increase. This is because buying the new car in the earlier year will produce writing down allowances in both years.

For example, if Harry buys a new model costing £40,000 with 75% business use and eligible for 18% writing down allowances, then buying it in 2020/21 will give rise to a writing down allowance of £5,400 this year (£40,000 x 18% x 75%). The unrelieved expenditure of £32,800 (£40,000 less 18%) carried forward will then give rise to a writing down allowance of £4,428 in 2021/22 (£32,800 x 18% x 75%).

Harry's total tax saving over the two years will then be £4,817 (£5,400 x 40% = £2,160 in 2020/21, plus £4,428 x 60% = £2,657 in 2021/22).

This is £1,577 better than the saving of £3,240 (£5,400 x 60%) in 2021/22 if he had postponed his purchase of the car until then.

Naturally, where the old car is being traded in for the new car, the two transactions will have to take place at the same time and it will be necessary to assess whether there still remains an overall saving to be made by postponing them. Usually there will be: for example, in Harry's case, postponing the sale saves an extra £2,035, whereas postponing the purchase reduces his savings by £1,577. Overall, postponing the trade-in saves him a net sum of £458.

But the best of all worlds (where possible) would be for Harry to buy his new car in 2020/21 and sell his old car in 2021/22.

Remember, it is postponing the sale of the old car that produces the tax saving, not postponing the purchase of the new car!

Some Words of Warning

Most sales of cars used in a business will produce a balancing allowance. Beware, however, that balancing charges may arise instead in some instances (especially sales of cars with very low CO_2 emissions). Where a balancing charge is likely to arise, it will generally be preferable to ensure the sale falls into a tax year where the landlord has a lower marginal Income Tax rate.

New cars with CO_2 emissions of no more than 50g/km currently attract 100% capital allowances (subject to an adjustment for private use). From April 2021, only new cars with zero emissions will qualify. In the March 2020 Budget, the Government announced that the 100% first year allowance for low-emission cars has been extended until 31st March 2025. It was initially due to end on 31st March 2021.

For more details on 'replacement of domestic items relief' and capital allowances claims for landlords, see the Taxcafe.co.uk guide *'How to Save Property Tax'*.

Claiming Mileage Rates Instead

In the above example, we assumed Harry claims capital allowances (and running costs) for the car used in his property business.

Individual landlords can now use the simpler mileage rates to claim tax relief for their business travel instead, if they wish.

For cars and vans the rates are 45p per mile for the first 10,000 miles and 25p per mile thereafter. For example, a landlord who travels 5,000 miles on business during the tax year may claim a deduction of £2,250 (5,000 x 45p).

Each landlord can make the choice between mileage rates and actual running costs (plus capital allowances) for each car or van. Once the choice is made, you must stick to it for the rest of the time you own that vehicle.

Self-Employed Business Owners

If you also own another unincorporated business, over and above your residential property business, you will have even more flexibility when it comes to postponing, or accelerating, your tax deductible expenses in order to save tax.

For example, a self-employed tree surgeon (who is also a landlord) may be able to postpone buying a new van if he or she thinks they will end up in a higher tax bracket next year.

This may be the case, for example, if the income from your other business has fallen sharply this year thanks to the coronavirus crisis but you expect it to be higher next year.

A self-employed web designer may be able to save tax by postponing new computer expenditure until next year... and so on.

Postponing tax deductible spending on either your property business or your other unincorporated business will achieve exactly the same result, which is to reduce your taxable income in a future tax year when your marginal tax rate is higher.

Chapter 13

Employing Family Members

If you have a partner, spouse, or child, it may be possible to employ them in your property business and pay them a salary which is less heavily taxed than your own income.

For example, you might employ your spouse to do repairs and maintenance work or pay one of your children to help with cleaning and other aspects of managing your portfolio.

As long as the salaries are not excessive and can be justified by the amount of work done, they will be a tax deductible expense for the property business.

In the case of children, you can generally only employ them if they are at least 13 years old (sometimes 14, depending on local by-laws) and, for all children under school leaving age, there are also legal limits on the amount of work they can do: which, in turn, limits the amount you can justify paying them.

Payments to family members must actually be made. Mere notional 'book entries' will not usually suffice. Spouses, partners and children aged 16 or more might subsequently make payments to you for 'room and board', and children might start paying for their own clothes, outings, meals out, etc, but these things are an entirely separate matter.

Tax savings can be achieved when the landlord has a higher tax rate than the family member they employ.

Tax savings are typically maximised when the landlord is a higher-rate taxpayer, paying tax at 40%, and the family member has no other income and can therefore be paid a tax-free salary.

The best tax savings are therefore often achieved when you employ children who are at school or university and have no other income.

When it comes to employing your spouse or partner, they may already have income from another job or business. This means it may not be possible to pay them a salary that is completely tax free. However, it may be possible to pay them a salary that is less heavily taxed than your own income.

In many cases the property business will be owned by the couple together. This means they cannot be employed and paid a salary (you cannot employ yourself in your own property business).

Reporting Requirements

Landlords don't usually have other employees so employing family members may require you to register for PAYE and report payments to HMRC under the Real Time Information system (RTI).

An accountancy firm will probably charge up to a few hundred pounds a year to run a small payroll.

Employers must register for PAYE and report under RTI where at least one employee:

- Earns more than the lower earnings limit (£6,240 this year), or
- Has another job

Where at least one employee meets the above criteria, the employer must report payments made to all employees.

If you don't already have a PAYE scheme and the family member is paid more than the lower earnings limit, or has another job, this may force you to operate a PAYE scheme.

If your business has no other employees, you don't have to operate PAYE and submit RTI returns if your children do not have other jobs and earn less than the lower earnings limit.

Tax-Free Salaries

The best outcome is when the family member can be paid a tax-free salary. By tax free, we mean with no income tax OR national insurance. Remember landlords do not themselves pay national insurance on their rental income. So if there's national insurance on a family member's salary, as well as income tax, the tax savings may become fairly modest, or disappear altogether.

Fortunately, it is often possible to pay family members, especially children who do not have any income from other sources, a fairly decent salary with no tax consequences:

- **Under 16.** Those aged under 16 can be paid up to £12,500 in 2020/21 with no income tax or national insurance.

- **16 to 20**. Children who are 16 and over have to pay 12% employee's national insurance on income over £9,500. However, there is no *employer's* national insurance payable as long as their income is below £50,000. This means your son or daughter can be paid £9,500 completely tax free this year and up to £12,500 with a total tax charge of just £360.

- **Children 21 and Over**. Children who are 21 and over can receive a completely tax-free salary of up to £8,788 this year. *Employer's* national insurance at the rate of 13.8% is payable on salaries over £8,788. However, most businesses, including property businesses, can claim the employment allowance. This covers the first £4,000 of employer's national insurance. This means most landlords can also pay children who are 21 and over a completely tax free salary of £9,500 this year and up to £12,500 with a total tax charge of just £360.

Second Jobs

It's quite possible that your child will have another part-time job, for example in a local restaurant or supermarket.

Even if your child has another job, it may be possible to pay them a completely tax free salary from your property business.

As long as both salaries, when added together, total less than £12,500 this year, there will be no income tax payable. Anything over will be taxed at 20%.

National insurance works differently. Employees can have more than one job with up to £9,500 of income from each job free from national insurance – as long as the businesses are not associated.

Remember, if your child has another job, you may have to register for PAYE and report their salary to HMRC. This could result in additional accountancy fees.

Bigger Salaries

In most cases the above tax-free salaries will comfortably cover part-time work done by your children in your property business at a commercially justifiable rate.

Where a bigger salary is justified, additional tax savings may be achieved if your own marginal tax rate is higher than that of your child – for example if you pay tax at 40% on your rental profits.

In most cases what you want to avoid is paying your child a salary that is subject to income tax (at 20%), employee's national insurance (at 12%) and employer's national insurance (at 13.8%).

Fortunately, most landlords will not have to pay employer's national insurance – the cost will be covered by the £4,000 employment allowance. The employment allowance will rarely be used up paying salaries to other employees because most landlords do not have other employees.

So in most cases the maximum amount of tax that will be paid on children's salaries will be 32%. Thus, where the landlord has a marginal tax rate of 40%, a small saving can still be achieved.

But where the landlord expects to be a basic-rate taxpayer this year, with a marginal tax rate of just 20%, a tax loss will be incurred by paying salaries to children that are taxed at 32%.

Example
Zachary is a landlord and a higher-rate taxpayer with a marginal tax rate of 40%. His 20 year old daughter Barbra is a full-time student and during her holidays Zachary employs her to help with cleaning, inventories and other admin. Her total pay comes to £5,000 in 2020/21. She does not receive any income from another job. Barbra does

not pay income tax or national insurance on this income. *Zachary is able to deduct Barbra's salary from his rental profits, saving him £2,000 in income tax, so the total tax saving is £2,000.*

Example
Tami is a landlord and a higher-rate taxpayer with a marginal tax rate of 40%. Her 18 year old son Jeff has another job at the local supermarket but also helps her out with the properties. This year she pays him £2,500 in total. Because Jeff's income from both jobs is less than £12,500 there is no income tax payable and because his salary is below the threshold no national insurance is payable. The total tax saving is £1,000 (£2,500 x 40%). However, because Jeff has another job Tami will have to register for PAYE and make regular submissions to HMRC. Employing a bookkeeper or firm of accountants could cost a few hundred pounds per year in additional fees.

Employing Your Spouse or Partner

In many families the properties will be owned by the couple with the rental profits split equally or in some other, perhaps more tax efficient, manner. Employing your spouse and paying them a salary is not relevant in these cases.

If your spouse or partner is not involved in the property business and does not have another job you can probably pay them a completely tax free salary of £9,500 this year and up to £12,500 with a total tax charge of just £360.

If your spouse or partner does have another job, which uses up their personal allowance, then any salary they receive from your property business will be taxed at 20% (40% once their total income exceeds £50,000).

National insurance works differently and your spouse or partner will be able to earn up to £9,500 from each job free from national insurance – as long as the businesses are not associated. After that they'll start paying 12% national insurance.

Once your spouse or partner is paying 20% income tax and 12% national insurance (32% altogether) there's not a huge amount to be gained by paying them additional salary in most circumstances. If you're a higher-rate taxpayer paying 40% tax on your rental profits the total saving will be 8%. Greater savings may be possible if you find yourself in a more heavily taxed bracket, for example £100,000-£125,000.

Spouse Has their Own Business

It's not always necessary to employ your spouse/partner in your property business. They may have a separate business of their own which you can hire to provide services to your property business.

Payments made to a family member who has their own existing business will need to include VAT if the business is VAT registered, or if the payments themselves push their gross annual income over the VAT registration threshold (currently £85,000). This will create an additional 20% VAT cost which the landlord will not be able to recover and would frequently mean that the payments have a detrimental effect overall.

Example
Belinda has a residential property portfolio that produces annual profits before interest of £60,000. Her interest costs total £20,000, giving her a true rental profit of £40,000. This means she would have been a basic-rate taxpayer before her mortgage tax relief was restricted.

She has two very young children plus an older child, Suzy, who is in full-time education. Belinda is therefore able to claim child benefit of £2,545 this year.

Her husband Dama has his own small business as an 'odd job man', producing an annual profit of around £30,000. He also carries out most of the repairs and maintenance work on Belinda's properties, but has never charged her for this.

While Belinda was a basic-rate taxpayer, it simply wasn't worth charging her: he would have paid a total of 29% in income tax and national insurance on the additional income, and she would have obtained tax relief at just 20% (as a basic-rate taxpayer), so there would have been an overall tax cost of 9%. (Belinda has, of course, always paid for any materials that were used.)

With all her mortgage interest now disallowed, Belinda has taxable income of £60,000. With this much taxable income, Belinda would lose all her child benefit and pay higher rate tax on £10,000.

To combat this, she employs Suzy part-time to help her in the business at an annual salary of £5,000. The salary is tax-free in Suzy's hands (as it is less than the national insurance threshold) but is tax deductible for Belinda.

Belinda also pays Dama £5,000 for repairs and maintenance work on her properties. The payment to Dama increases his total tax and national insurance liability by £1,450 (£5,000 x 29%), but leads to greater savings for Belinda. In fact, her total savings created by the payments to Suzy and Dama are as follows:

Child benefit saved	*£2,545*
Higher rate tax relief (£10,000 x 40%)	*£4,000*
Total saving	*£6,545*

Belinda continues to remain a basic-rate taxpayer and thus protects herself from the interest relief restriction.

It has cost the family £1,450 (the extra tax and national insurance paid by Dama) but they are still £5,095 better off overall. Annual savings at a similar level could continue for as long as Suzy has no other income of her own (they will reduce when she is no longer eligible for child benefit).

Thereafter, Belinda will still save tax by continuing to pay Dama for his repairs and maintenance work: as long as her marginal tax rate remains higher than his, the payments will be worthwhile.

Unlike some of the 'one-off' items discussed in Chapter 12, payments to a spouse or partner may provide a means to continue saving tax consistently year on year.

Payments to children are generally a less permanent solution. Eventually, Suzy will probably have some taxable income of her own and the saving will diminish.

Payments to Family and the Coronavirus Crisis

With most schools and universities having closed early, there has never been a better time to employ your children in your business… at least in theory.

I say in theory because, at the time of writing, many businesses were closed or operating only partially.

In the current environment landlords should also be careful about paying salaries to family members before calculating their own marginal tax rate.

For example, where a landlord has experienced a significant drop in income (either from their property business or another job or business) it's possible their marginal tax rate will have fallen from, say, 40% to 20%. In this case, there is no point paying a salary to a family member who will pay tax at, say, 32%.

Chapter 14

Increasing Tax Deductible Expenses

A very easy way to save tax is simply to increase your business expenditure. But this, in itself, would be pointless, because...

Bayley's Law
The truly wise investor does not seek merely to minimise the amount of tax payable, but rather to maximise the amount of wealth remaining after all taxes have been accounted for.

In other words, the sensible objective is generally to increase your profit after tax rather than simply reducing your tax bill. Going out and spending extra money on your business just to save tax is usually nonsense. This is why most of our advice regarding expenditure is about the timing of the expenditure, or the type of expenditure, and not about spending extra money just for the sake of it.

But there are a few exceptions where additional expenditure may be justified.

In Chapter 12, we looked at some of the discretionary expenditure on your properties that may enhance the value of the property, or its rental yield, and yet still be allowed as deductible repairs expenditure.

In Chapter 13, we looked at payments to family members that legitimately increase your tax deductible expenditure, but also keep more of your money 'in the family'.

Here are a few other ideas:

Property Management Fees

Some landlords have entered into arrangements whereby they pay property management fees to some sort of connected entity, such as their own company, a family partnership, or a spouse or partner.

Generally, we feel these arrangements are highly risky, as they lack any commercial substance. Where, however, the connected entity has a genuine property management business, with other unconnected clients, the arrangement may be valid.

Having unconnected employees (i.e. non-family members) within the property management business would also give it more validity.

In Chapter 27, we will look at the potential benefits of using your own property management company for this purpose. For property management fees paid to a spouse, partner or other relative, the situation will be much the same as in Dama's case in the example set out in Chapter 13.

Whatever type of entity is used, there are two words of warning we must emphasise:

i)   The management fees charged must not exceed a normal commercial rate and should not exceed the rate charged to other, unconnected, clients (they can be less, however).

ii)   If the total management fees (from all sources) received by the entity in any twelve month period exceed the VAT registration threshold (fixed at £85,000 until 31st March 2022), he/she/it will need to register for VAT and charge 20% on their fees. This will generally eliminate most, if not all, of any advantage gained through the arrangement.

Other Tax Deductible Spending

There are a number of tax deductible items that often get overlooked. For landlords with a marginal tax rate of just 20%, it may seem unnecessarily complex or burdensome to worry about these things when the potential tax savings are small.

However, with many landlords' marginal tax rates increasing to 40% or more because of the mortgage tax change, it may perhaps be a good idea to review some of these items. It is not a case of spending any more money, merely a case of being more meticulous about claiming the expenditure you are already incurring.

Some of the things we would recommend you consider are:

- Use of home (even the most minor business use of your own home will generally entitle you to claim an annual deduction of £104; much bigger claims are often justifiable in many cases)

- Motor expenses (are you recording and claiming for all your business journeys?)

- Capital allowances on equipment and cars (see Chapter 12 for more information)

- Travel and subsistence costs

- Telephone, broadband and other IT expenses

More information on all these types of expenditure, and on how much you are entitled to claim, is provided in the Taxcafe.co.uk guide *'How to Save Property Tax'*.

Self-Employed Business Owners

Finally, it's worth pointing out again that if you own another unincorporated business, over and above your residential property business, you will have even more flexibility when it comes to increasing your tax deductible expenses in order to save tax. For example, it may be easier to employ family members in your other business rather than in your property business.

Increasing tax deductible spending on either business will achieve exactly the same result for Income Tax purposes, which is to reduce your taxable income now that the tax relief on your mortgage interest has been reduced.

Increasing the spending in your other, non-property, business will usually save National Insurance too!

Chapter 15

Accelerating Tax Relief for Finance Costs

In Chapter 12, we looked at the potential benefits of postponing tax deductible expenditure so that it falls into a tax year in which you have a higher marginal tax rate.

For finance costs, it could be worth doing the opposite and accelerating costs because, from 2020/21 onwards, they only attract tax relief at 20%.

Interest is a time-based cost, so it will seldom be possible for it to be accelerated. But there might be opportunities to accelerate other finance costs, such as loan arrangement fees, broker's fees, and professional costs incurred in obtaining a mortgage.

"But, wait," I hear you say, "it's too late to accelerate these costs to before 2020/21."

That, of course, is true, but it may not be too late to accelerate the accounting, or tax relief, for these costs. (For full details of the treatment of loan arrangement fees and other items that may be claimed as costs of raising long-term finance, as well as the rules for claiming these costs over the useful life of the relevant loan under traditional 'accruals basis' accounting, see the Taxcafe.co.uk guide *'How to Save Property Tax'*.)

The tax return for 2019/20 is not due until 31st January 2021 and can be amended at any time until 31st January 2022; the tax return for 2018/19 can be amended at any time until 31st January 2021. Hence, it is still possible to make changes to your tax returns for either of these years, and this could provide you with a better rate of tax relief on your finance costs.

Effective Rates of Tax Relief on Finance Costs

For a typical higher-rate taxpayer with a marginal tax rate of 40%, the effective rate of relief for finance costs is generally as follows:

2018/19:   30%
2019/20:   25%
2020/21:   20%

For a higher-rate taxpayer with total taxable income over £100,000, who is suffering the withdrawal of their personal allowance and a marginal tax rate of 60%, the effective rate of relief is:

2018/19:   40%   (taxable income from £100,000 to £123,700)
2019/20:   30%   (taxable income from £100,000 to £125,000)
2020/21:   20%   (regardless of taxable income)

For an additional rate taxpayer with total taxable income over £150,000 and a marginal tax rate of 45%, the effective rate of relief is:

2018/19:   32.5%
2019/20:   26.25%
2020/21:   20%

Hence, for many taxpayers, accelerating the accounting, or tax relief, for finance costs will produce considerable savings.

Accelerating Finance Costs with the Cash Basis

Firstly, if your total annual rental income (from *either* UK property or overseas property) is no more than £150,000, you may be able to bring more of these costs into an earlier year simply by using the cash basis of accounting (see Chapter 28). Landlords using the cash basis are generally able to claim all their finance costs *as they are paid* (subject to the tax relief restriction that is the focus of this guide).

Example
Omar is a higher-rate taxpayer. In July 2018, he took out an interest only buy-to-let mortgage with a 20 year term. He incurred a loan arrangement fee and various other related costs totalling £4,800.

Initially, Omar submitted his 2018/19 tax return based on traditional 'accruals basis' accounting. He therefore claimed just one twentieth of his July 2018 finance costs, £240 (£4,800/20). He was intending to claim the same amount in 2019/20 and every year thereafter, for the next eighteen years. This would have produced tax relief as follows:

2018/19 - £240 @ 30%   *£72*
2019/20 - £240 @ 25%   *£60*
2020/21 to 2037/38:
£240 x 18 @ 20%   *£864*
Total: *£996*

However, Omar now amends his 2018/19 tax return and elects to use the cash basis of accounting, meaning he can claim his entire cost of £4,800 in 2018/19, providing tax relief at an effective rate of 30% on the whole amount, worth £1,440 (£4,800 x 30%).

While there are many other factors Omar should take into account (and we will examine these in Chapter 28), changing to the cash basis for 2018/19 has provided him with an extra £444 (£1,440 – £996) worth of tax relief on his finance costs.

Furthermore, his tax relief has been considerably accelerated and will now produce an immediate cash saving, rather than savings over twenty years!

Accelerating Finance Costs under Traditional 'Accruals Basis' Accounting

Even if you are not eligible to use the cash basis, or do not wish to do so, you may still be able to accelerate tax relief for some of your finance costs.

This is due to the fact that, under traditional 'accruals basis' accounting, loan arrangement fees and other costs associated with obtaining a mortgage or long-term loan must generally be claimed over the **useful** life of that loan. Many landlords, however, mistakenly claim these costs over the **legal** life of the loan.

Example

Sharona is a full-time landlord with total taxable income of £120,000 (and thus a marginal tax rate of 60%) in both 2018/19 and 2019/20. This is before accounting for a loan arrangement fee and related costs totalling £20,000 that she incurred when she refinanced her residential property portfolio in May 2018. She is not eligible to use the cash basis of accounting.

Sharona's new finance consists of a twenty year fixed-term loan secured over her portfolio. Before reading this guide, she was planning to claim her £20,000 of finance costs over the life of the loan, despite the fact she always fully intended to refinance her portfolio again in 2020/21, just after the initial two year period (with a reduced interest rate) expired.

Following this method, she would end up claiming £1,000 in 2018/19 and 2019/20 and the balance of £18,000 in 2020/21. The value of her tax relief would be as follows:

2018/19 - £1,000 @ 40% =   £400
2019/20 - £1,000 @ 30% =   £300
2020/21 - £18,000 @ 20% =   £3,600
Total: £4,300

However, having read this guide (and being surprised to find herself in it), Sharona realises she may legitimately claim these costs over two years, i.e. £10,000 per year in 2018/19 and 2019/20. She amends her 2018/19 tax return accordingly and this new method produces tax relief as follows:

2018/19 - £10,000 @ 40% =   £4,000
2019/20 - £10,000 @ 30% =   £3,000
Total: £7,000

Not only does she obtain tax relief earlier, she also enjoys £2,700 of additional savings.

When claiming loan arrangement fees and other associated costs over a shorter period than the legal life of the loan, it is essential to record and retain evidence of your logic for doing so: i.e. the reasons you believe the **useful** life of the loan is shorter than the **legal** life of the loan.

Amending Tax Returns

Amending a previous year's tax return is a relatively straightforward matter and may be used to make a number of claims, elections, etc, that might not initially have seemed desirable, or which might simply have been missed: including opting into, or out of, the cash basis.

A previous year's tax return may also be amended in order to implement or increase claims for business expenditure that has previously been missed or understated, including loan arrangement fees and other finance costs.

Amendments to a previous year's tax return under this simple procedure are quite commonplace and can be seen as a normal part of the self-assessment regime.

However, it is important to bear in mind that amending a previous year's tax return means it is open for enquiry once again (for a period of twelve months) and HMRC may investigate any aspect of the return. While this should not prevent legitimate claims being made, it is something that should be borne in mind.

Chapter 16

Pension Contributions

A simple way for landlords to beat the mortgage tax increase is by upping their pension contributions. How much extra will you need to invest to claw back all the extra tax you will pay? As a rule of thumb, your *gross* pension contribution will need to be half as big as your mortgage interest. So if you have £10,000 of buy-to-let interest, you'll typically need to make a gross pension contribution of £5,000 to recover the extra tax you'll pay.

Example – Before Pension Contribution
Usman earns £40,000 as a self-employed consultant and a rental profit of £10,000 from some residential properties (after deducting £10,000 of buy-to-let interest). If Usman's mortgage tax relief was NOT restricted he would have total taxable income of £50,000 and his total after-tax income would be:

£50,000 income - £7,500 tax = £42,500

However, with his mortgage interest no longer tax deductible, Usman's Income Tax bill will increase by £2,000 to £9,500 (he'll have an extra £10,000 taxed at 40% but will also be entitled to a 20% tax reduction). In summary, his after-tax income will fall from £42,500 to £40,500.

(Usman's National Insurance has been ignored for simplicity.)

Example – After Pension Contribution
Usman decides to invest £4,000 in his pension. The taxman will add £1,000 of basic-rate tax relief, giving him a gross pension contribution of £5,000. He will also receive higher-rate tax relief through his self-assessment tax computation. This is calculated as 20% of his gross pension contribution: £5,000 x 20% = £1,000.

In total Usman enjoys £2,000 tax relief by making a £5,000 gross pension contribution (a cash contribution of £4,000). Hence, all the extra tax arising due to the reduction in his interest relief is clawed back by making a gross pension contribution half as big as his mortgage interest payments.

Pensions: Cashflow Issues

Although you can completely reverse the mortgage tax increase by making pension contributions, there is one significant problem: your money is locked away until you reach the minimum retirement age (currently 55). In other words, pension contributions can seriously damage your cashflow!

We saw that Usman's disposable income will fall from £42,500 to £40,500 when his mortgage tax relief is fully restricted. By making a pension contribution he claws back £2,000 and ends up with £42,500 again BUT £5,000 of that is stuck inside a pension plan! His actual disposable income will fall by a further £3,000 to £37,500. Usman's financial position is summarised below:

Usman: Tax Relief versus Cash Flow

	No Pension Contribution	Pension Contribution
	£	£
Self-employment income	40,000	40,000
Taxable rental profit	20,000	20,000
	---------	---------
	60,000	60,000
Less:		
Income tax	9,500[1]	8,500[2]
Pension contribution	0	4,000
Mortgage interest[3]	10,000	10,000
Disposable income[4]	**40,500**	**37,500**
Pension Pot	**0**	**5,000**

Notes
1. First £12,500 tax free, next £37,500 taxed at 20%, final £10,000 taxed at 40%. Reduced by £2,000 tax reduction (mortgage interest x 20%).
2. Further reduced by £1,000 higher-rate tax relief on pension contribution.
3. Taxable rental profit is not the same as actual rental profit; his £10,000 of mortgage interest must be deducted to calculate his true disposable income.
4. Ignores National Insurance payments. These would be the same under both scenarios and hence do not alter the overall conclusion.

Why does Usman's disposable income fall by £3,000? Because he personally invests £4,000 into his pension but gets £1,000 of higher-rate relief through his self-assessment tax computation.

In summary, for every £10,000 of mortgage interest you pay you will generally be able to claw back the extra tax you will face as a higher-rate taxpayer by making a £5,000 gross pension contribution. £3,000 will ultimately come from you and £2,000 from the taxman. Thus, your disposable income will also fall by a further £3,000.

Protecting Your Child Benefit

So far we've looked at the "bread and butter" case where the landlord is a regular higher-rate taxpayer and enjoys 40% tax relief on the pension contributions. Some landlords may be able to enjoy even more tax relief.

Take Usman, for example. His taxable income has risen from £50,000 (before the tax change) to £60,000 this year.

With income over £50,000 he will end up paying the child benefit charge if he is a parent and the highest earner in the household. In this case a pension contribution will reduce his "adjusted net income" which will also reduce the child benefit charge.

For example, a £5,000 gross pension contribution will reduce his adjusted net income from £60,000 to £55,000 which means his child benefit charge will be halved from £2,545 to £1,272 (if he has three children, based on current rates). In total, Usman will enjoy £3,273 tax relief on his £5,000 pension contribution, i.e. 65.5% tax relief.

Other Important Tax Thresholds

If your taxable income gets pushed over the £100,000 tax threshold this year, you will also start losing your personal allowance. Once your taxable income reaches £125,000, your personal allowance will be completely withdrawn.

Making pension contributions will reduce your adjusted net income, which means you will also recover some of your personal allowance, as well as enjoying the regular pension tax reliefs.

As a result, making pension contributions while your taxable income is in the £100,000-£125,000 tax bracket will generally attract 60% tax relief this year.

When your taxable income rises above £150,000 you become an additional-rate taxpayer and start paying tax at 45% on most types of income. The flipside is you can enjoy 45% tax relief on your pension contributions.

However, some additional-rate taxpayers face greater restrictions to their pension contributions than other taxpayers. Your annual allowance – the maximum amount that can be invested in a pension each year – could be reduced from £40,000 to just £4,000.

Fortunately, following an announcement in the March 2020 Budget, this pension taper now only kicks in at much higher income levels than previously. As a result, many high earners can benefit from much higher pension contributions than before.

(See the Taxcafe.co.uk guide *'Pension Magic'* for further details.)

Pension Contributions & the Coronavirus

Preserving Your Cash

The problem with pensions is your money is locked up until you reach age 55 (possibly rising to 57 in 2028).

If you're under 55, before making significant pension contributions you should make sure you have other resources to protect against:

- Unforeseen expenses, and an
- Unforeseen drop in income.

For many individuals the coronavirus crisis has resulted in an unforeseen drop in income. Anyone worried about the state of their finances may therefore wish to consider reducing or halting their pension contributions for a while.

Although this may result in a higher tax bill during the current tax year, many people will be able to completely reverse this tax increase by making bigger contributions in future tax years.

Even if you're 55 or older you cannot get your hands on all your pension contributions immediately without incurring a penalty. So if you're 55 or older you may also wish to consider reducing or halting your contributions for a while.

Reducing your pension contributions does not mean you have to stop saving. There are other places you can put your savings!

There are some risks and practical issues when it comes to postponing pension contributions, especially if you belong to a workplace pension scheme and this means giving up the contribution you receive from your employer. See the Taxcafe guide *'Pension Magic'* for further details.

Protecting Higher-Rate Tax Relief

Another reason why it may be a good idea to reduce or postpone your pension contributions is to protect your higher-rate tax relief if you expect your income to fall during the current tax year.

For the current 2020/21 tax year, if your taxable income is more than £50,000 you can enjoy higher-rate tax relief on your pension contributions. If your income is less than £50,000 all you will get is basic-rate tax relief.

If you think you will be a basic-rate taxpayer this year but expect to be a higher-rate taxpayer in the future you may be better off postponing your pension contributions until then.

If a basic-rate taxpayer postpones making pension contributions until they become a higher-rate taxpayer, they can boost the total amount saved by up to 33%.

Pension Contributions – Other Issues

When it comes to making pension contributions there are lots of things you need to remember, including:

- **Do you have earnings?** Everyone under 75 can make a gross pension contribution of up to £3,600 per year. If you want to contribute more your gross contributions must not exceed your annual earnings. Salaries and trading profits are earnings for this purpose; rental profits generally are not. If you want to make big pension contributions you must have earnings from other sources.

- **The £40,000 Annual Allowance.** Total pension contributions by you and your employer must generally not exceed £40,000 per year, although you can sometimes carry forward unused allowance from earlier tax years.

- **The Lifetime Allowance.** Additional restrictions apply where the total value of all your pension schemes, including the value of any benefits under schemes run by your employer, exceeds the lifetime allowance. The lifetime allowance is £1,073,100 for 2020/21.

- **Is Tax Only Deferred and Not Saved?** Subject to the 25% tax-free lump sum, withdrawals from your pension scheme will be taxable. Arguably, therefore, your pension contributions are only deferring tax rather than saving it. However, much of this depends on how you time your withdrawals and on what your income situation is at the time; so absolute savings are still possible if you get your timing right!

This is just a brief overview. For more information see the Taxcafe.co.uk guide *'Pension Magic'*.

Chapter 17

Should You Reduce Your Buy-to-Let Mortgages?

Many landlords have asked whether they should reduce their mortgages now that tax relief on their interest has been reduced.

Reducing your buy-to-let debt does not solve the fundamental problem you may face thanks to this tax change: an increase in your taxable income, with more of that income taxed at higher rates.

Paying down debt may actually *increase* your tax bill, not reduce it – if your interest payments get smaller, your 20% basic-rate tax reduction will also get smaller.

Paying down debt may, nevertheless, lead to an increase in your after-tax disposable income if you can't get a better return elsewhere on your surplus cash. There are, of course, other things you can do with your surplus cash including:

- Keep it in a tax-free savings account
- Pay down other debts (e.g. the mortgage on your home)
- Use it to fund further property purchases

If your savings are kept in an ISA the interest will, of course, be tax free. And even if not, the personal savings allowance exempts the first £1,000 of interest from tax if you are a basic-rate taxpayer (£500 if you're a higher-rate taxpayer).

Even though it may be tax free, the interest you can earn on your savings is usually lower than the interest you pay on your borrowings, so you are usually better off using your savings to reduce your debt.

You could also use your savings to reduce any personal debt you have. Interest rates on credit cards and most short-term borrowings are generally much higher than mortgage rates and usually enjoy no tax relief whatsoever, so it is usually most efficient to pay off these debts first.

If you don't have any short-term borrowings you could use any surplus cash you have to reduce the mortgage on your home, if you have one. Interest rates on buy-to-let mortgages are generally higher than the interest rates on home loans and the product fees are often higher too. So at first glance it would appear that paying off buy-to-let debt is a better idea.

However, because buy-to-let interest enjoys tax relief, you may find that the mortgage on your home is actually more expensive and should be repaid first.

Remember that you may incur early repayment charges when you pay off certain types of mortgage debt. This may affect your decision to repay one debt rather than another.

Calculating the Real Cost of Buy-to-Let Interest

Before you pay off any of your buy-to-let debt you should calculate its true after-tax cost. For example, let's say you have a £100,000 buy-to-let mortgage and the interest rate is 3%. Your annual interest bill will be £3,000 and you will enjoy £600 of tax relief:

$$£3,000 \text{ x } 20\% \text{ basic-rate tax reduction} = £600$$

The true cost of the loan is therefore £2,400, i.e. 2.4%. So if the interest on your personal debt (e.g. the mortgage on your home) is *more than* 2.4% you should pay off your personal debt first. Otherwise you should pay off your buy-to-let mortgage first.

Example
Rees is a higher-rate taxpayer who has £10,000 sitting in a cash ISA earning 1% tax free – £100 per year.

He has a mortgage on his home on which he is paying 2% interest. So if he uses his £10,000 of ISA savings to reduce his home mortgage he will save £200 per year in interest.

He also has a buy-to-let mortgage on which he is paying 3%. If he uses his ISA savings to reduce this debt he will save £300 per year in interest. However, he will also lose £60 of tax relief (£300 x 20% tax reduction). So his net saving will be £240.

The best option for Rees is therefore to pay off his buy-to-let debt.

Protecting Your Cash

In theory, you are almost always better off using your spare cash to reduce your debt.

Although this may be the "optimal" route, a prudent landlord should maintain a healthy cash reserve to protect against unexpected drops in rental income and unforeseen expenses.

Having a healthy cash buffer is especially important in the current climate.

In fact, instead of reducing mortgages, many landlords have recently been taking payment holidays of several months.

I know one landlord who is doing this, even though his tenants are mostly up to date with their rent, so that he can build a cash reserve to use in his property business.

Taking a mortgage holiday is not without drawbacks. Recent media reports have claimed that landlords on payment holidays have been rejected for mortgages to buy new properties.

Chapter 18

Selling Property

It's unlikely many landlords will take the "nuclear option" and sell their properties because their mortgage tax relief has reduced – most, we suspect, will simply take the tax hit on the chin.

For most landlords, investing in property has become less profitable but not necessarily *unprofitable* – many will probably continue to enjoy a positive rental profit (unless interest rates increase significantly) and will probably still see property as the best way to accumulate wealth.

Remember returns from property come in two flavours: rental income and capital growth. Many landlords will be willing to pay more Income Tax if they're enjoying an even higher amount of capital growth.

Even if property prices increase by just one or two per cent per year over the long term, many landlords will still end up better off overall, despite the loss of some of their tax relief. Of course capital growth is not guaranteed and property prices can and do fall.

Unfortunately not all landlords are in such a happy situation. Some, in particular those with large portfolios with lots of debt, may suffer such a sharp decline in income they may be forced to sell up. Before we take a look at a few examples, let's remind ourselves how Capital Gains Tax is calculated.

Capital Gains Tax Basics

If you sell a rental property you could end up paying Capital Gains Tax. For a full discussion of this complex tax we recommend reading the Taxcafe.co.uk guide *'How to Save Property Tax'*.

Essentially you pay Capital Gains Tax on your profit, which is generally the difference between the price you paid for the property and the price you sell it for. You can also deduct your buying and selling costs from your profit, typically Stamp Duty Land Tax, estate agent fees and legal fees. You can also deduct the cost of any improvements you have made to the property (but not repairs – see Chapter 12). Finally, you can deduct the Capital Gains Tax annual exemption (£12,300 in 2020/21).

This leaves you with your taxable gain, which is taxed at 28% if you are a higher-rate taxpayer and 18% to the extent your basic-rate band is not used up by your income. For most assets these Capital Gains Tax rates have been reduced to 20% and 10% respectively but NOT for residential property.

Those thinking of selling properties may wish to consider selling those that have the smallest capital gains, although, naturally, there are lots of other factors that may affect this decision.

Landlord Suffers Rental Loss

One group of landlords who may decide to scale back their portfolios are those who don't depend on their properties for rental income but, thanks to the interest tax change, end up making rental losses on some of their properties.

Example
Anna is a higher-rate taxpayer who works full time and also owns two rental properties. She doesn't rely on the properties for income but isn't prepared to accept rental losses ("Investments aren't supposed to lose you money, especially when they take up so much of your time").

The second property was purchased a few years ago for £200,000, using a £150,000 buy-to-let mortgage and by borrowing £50,000 against the first property.

Let's say she receives net rental income of £10,000 per year from the second property. This is after deducting all her costs except mortgage interest which comes to £8,000 per year. With a taxable rental profit of £2,000, she paid £800 Income Tax in 2016/17 (before the mortgage tax change), resulting in a £1,200 after-tax rental profit on this property.

Assuming rent and interest rates remained the same, the after-tax rental profit on the second property would have fallen to £800 in 2017/18, £400 in 2018/19, £0 in 2019/20, and she'll incur a loss of £400 in 2020/21. Her after-tax profits have fallen as the tax relief on her mortgage interest has been gradually reduced.

Because Anna is making a rental loss, in the absence of any increase in the rent she can charge, she must rely on capital growth to make the investment worthwhile.

Fortunately, even if the property only increases in value by one or two per cent per year this will more than compensate for her £400 rental loss. For example, if the property rises by just two per cent per year she will enjoy an annual capital gain of at least £4,000.

Of course, capital gains are by no means guaranteed and the property could fall in value.

If Anna decides to sell the property this year and receives more than £200,000 for it, she may be subject to Capital Gains Tax. For example, let's assume that, after deducting all her buying and selling costs, she is left with a gain of £30,000.

After deducting the £12,300 annual Capital Gains Tax exemption this will leave her with a taxable gain of £17,700 and a tax bill of £4,956 (£17,700 x 28%).

Anna sells the property to stem her rental loss, but the Capital Gains Tax bill is more than 12 times bigger than her annual rental loss!

Clearly, deciding whether a property should be sold is a complex matter and would need to be based on many factors – not just a rental loss in one year. Anna will need to think about where she sees rents, interest rates and property prices going in the years ahead. Unfortunately all of these are impossible to predict!

Nevertheless, many landlords who end up with modest rental losses may decide to hold onto their properties because, being an optimistic bunch, most believe rents and capital values will continue to rise over the long term.

Landlord Suffers Huge Drop in Income

Those most likely to sell are landlords who depend on their properties for income AND are seeing their income fall sharply now that their mortgage tax relief has been reduced. Those most at risk of this happening are landlords who have big property portfolios but also large amounts of debt.

Example

Remember Katerina from Case Study 6 in Chapter 6 who owns the heavily geared property portfolio? With her interest no longer tax deductible, her taxable rental profit rises from £50,000 to £125,000. Not only does she end up paying tax at 40%, she also loses her child benefit and Income Tax personal allowance. As a result, her after-tax income falls from £45,000 to £22,500 – a drop of 50%.

Katerina can no longer pay the household bills and decides to sell 60% of her properties. As a result, her taxable income will also fall by 60%, from £125,000 back to £50,000. She will no longer be subject to 40% tax and will keep all her child benefit and Income Tax personal allowance. The first £12,500 of her income will be tax free and the remainder will be taxed at 20%, giving her a tax bill of £7,500.

What about her interest payments? Let's assume her portfolio is worth around £2.67 million and she has 75% buy-to-let mortgages totalling £2 million. This means her total equity is around £670,000.

To give Katerina the best outcome possible we'll assume she does not have to pay any Capital Gains Tax on the properties she sells – we'll assume they've barely risen in value since she bought them.

If she sells 60% of her properties, her debt will fall by 60% from £2 million to £800,000. Furthermore, she will also release 60% of her equity (roughly £400,000), which can be used to reduce the debt on her remaining properties. As a result, her total debt will fall by 80% to £400,000, which means her interest payments will also fall by 80% from £75,000 to £15,000.

Her interest payments are no longer tax deductible but she is entitled to a 20% tax reduction, which amounts to £3,000, giving her a final Income Tax bill of £4,500.

Katerina's after-tax disposable income is calculated as follows:

	£
Net rental income	*50,000*
Child benefit	*2,500*
Less: Interest	*15,000*
Less: Tax	*4,500*
After-tax income	*33,000*

By selling 60% of her properties, Katerina has managed to increase her after-tax income by over £10,000: from £22,500 to £33,000.

However, she's still £12,000 short of the £45,000 she would have made if her interest payments were fully tax deductible. Furthermore, she will also lose out on a lot of capital growth if the properties she sold would have risen in value in the years ahead.

To cover the £12,000 black hole in her income Katerina may need to find a part-time job or start another business. Hopefully with a much smaller property portfolio she will have more time on her hands to do this!

Chapter 19

Company Owners with Dividend Income

If you are a company owner and separately own mortgaged rental properties personally you will have to be careful about the amount of dividend income you pay yourself if you want to avoid going over the various tax thresholds.

This is one of the main tax benefits of being a company owner. Unlike regular salaried employees or owners of unincorporated businesses (e.g. sole traders), company owners can control the amount of income they receive and therefore control their personal Income Tax bills.

Many company owners pay themselves a small tax-free salary and take the rest of their income as dividends (because there is no National Insurance on dividends).

The first £2,000 of dividend income you receive is tax free thanks to the "dividend allowance". All taxpayers, regardless of the level of their income, receive this allowance.

For those receiving dividends in excess of the dividend allowance, the following Income Tax rates apply:

Basic-rate taxpayers	7.5%
Higher-rate taxpayers	32.5%
Additional-rate taxpayers	38.1%

Dividends are always treated as the top slice of your income and are therefore subject to the highest possible tax rate.

The reduced tax relief on mortgage interest means many landlords now have bigger taxable rental profits.

This in turn has pushed more of the dividend income they receive from their companies over the higher-rate threshold where it is subject to the 32.5% tax rate.

Example

Sinead owns a graphic design company and pays herself a salary of £12,500 and dividends of £40,000.

She's also a landlord and earns a rental profit of £35,500 <u>before</u> deducting her interest costs. She pays £12,000 interest on her buy-to-let mortgages, so her true rental profit is £23,500. However, with none of her mortgage interest tax deductible any more, her <u>taxable</u> rental profit will be £35,500. Along with her salary of £12,500 this will take her income up to £48,000.

Because this is still below the £50,000 higher-rate threshold all of her taxable rental profit will be taxed at 20%, with an offsetting tax reduction of 20% of her mortgage interest. So at first glance it looks like she is unaffected by the change to interest tax relief.

Where Sinead will feel the sting is on her dividend income. Dividends are always treated as the top slice of income. The first £2,000 of her dividend income will be tax free thanks to the dividend allowance but this will take her income up to the £50,000 higher-rate threshold.

All her remaining dividend income will therefore be taxed at the 32.5% higher rate.

The end result is that, because her taxable rental profits are £12,000 higher than her true rental profit, this will push £12,000 of her dividend income over the higher-rate threshold where it will be taxed at 32.5% instead of 7.5% – an increase of 25%.

Thus her final tax bill will increase by £3,000 (£12,000 x 25%) compared with what it would be if her interest was fully deductible.

Many company owners who are also landlords will find themselves in a similar position and will see their tax bills increase by an amount equivalent to 25% of their mortgage interest (compared with the position if their interest was fully deductible).

For example, a company owner with £20,000 of buy-to-let interest could end up paying £5,000 more tax from 2020/21 onwards.

Tax Planning for Company Owners

Company owners who separately own mortgaged rental properties personally have to be careful about the amount of dividend income they pay themselves if they want to avoid paying 32.5% tax.

Example
Jessie owns a small engineering company and some rental property.

Because she earns rental income she decides to pay herself a salary of £8,788 in 2020/21. (See the Taxcafe guide 'Salary versus Dividends' for an explanation as to why this may be the optimal salary for someone with income from other sources.)

Her rental property produces income of £20,000 net of all expenses except mortgage interest. Her mortgage interest is £7,500 so her true rental profit is £12,500.

However, her taxable rental profit is £20,000 and it is this number she must use when deciding how much dividend income to take.

With a salary of £8,788 and taxable rental profit of £20,000 Jessie can pay herself a dividend of up to £21,212 before she becomes a higher-rate taxpayer and has to pay 32.5% tax (£50,000 - £8,788 - £20,000).

Example
Cillian owns a software company and a portfolio of rental properties. Because he earns rental income he decides to pay himself a salary of £8,788 in 2020/21.

His rental property produces income of £50,000 (net of all expenses except interest). His mortgage interest is £15,000 so his true rental profit is £35,000. However, his taxable rental profit is £50,000.

With a salary of £8,788 and taxable rental profit of £50,000 Cillian is a higher-rate taxpayer and will pay 32.5% tax on his dividend income (except the first £2,000 which is always tax free).

Cillian can pay himself a dividend of up to £41,212 before he reaches the £100,000 tax threshold where his personal allowance will be gradually withdrawn. He will then pay tax at an effective rate of 52.5% on the next £25,000 of dividend income he receives (see the Taxcafe guide 'Salary versus Dividends' for an explanation).

Other Important Tax Thresholds

If her company has enough profits to distribute, Jessie in the above example may decide to pay herself a dividend of more than £21,212 this year, even though she will have to pay 32.5% tax on the additional income.

If she receives child benefit and is the highest earner in her household she may also be subject to the child benefit charge when her taxable income goes above £50,000.

The child benefit charge creates the following marginal tax rates on dividend income in the £50,000-£60,000 tax bracket:

Children	Marginal Tax Rate on Dividends
1	43%
2	51%
3	58%
4	65%

Plus 7% for each additional child

Income under £100,000 this Year

Some company owners who separately own rental properties personally may see their incomes dip below £100,000 this year, for example if their rental income has fallen because of the coronavirus crisis.

They may then wish to consider upping their company dividends (where profits allow) if they think their taxable income will rise above £100,000 in a future tax year.

Once your income rises above £100,000, your personal allowance is gradually withdrawn. At this point you could end up paying Income Tax at an effective rate of over 50% on some of your dividend income.

So paying 32.5% now may be preferable, even if you do not need the income immediately.

Some of the money can be lent back to the company if necessary.

Distributable Profits

Companies can only pay dividends to the extent that they have distributable profits available, as evidenced by a suitable set of accounts. Gains arising on property revaluations do not represent distributable profits for this purpose.

For more information on the limitations and formalities applying to the payment of dividends, see the Taxcafe.co.uk guide *'Salary versus Dividends'*.

Chapter 20

Emigration

If you decide to retire or work abroad you will still have to pay UK Income Tax on your rental properties situated in the UK. However, once you become non-resident it's possible the reduction in interest tax relief will affect you much less or not at all. This will typically be the case if the only UK income you have is from UK properties.

Example – UK Resident
Dennis is a UK resident with a salary of £60,000. He also has rental income of £40,000 and property expenses of £6,000, so his taxable rental profit is £34,000. He pays £14,000 in mortgage interest but none of this is deductible when calculating his taxable rental profit.

With this much salary Dennis is a higher-rate taxpayer and will pay 40% tax on the £34,000 taxable rental profit – £13,600. He will also receive a tax reduction equal to 20% of his interest – £2,800. Thus in total he pays £10,800 tax on his rental income.

Example revised – Non-Resident
This time we will assume Dennis is non-resident. He still earns a salary of £60,000 but none of this is taxable in the UK. With no other UK income the first £12,500 of his £34,000 taxable rental profit will be tax free. Income Tax at 20% will be payable on the remainder, and this amounts to £4,300. He will also enjoy a tax reduction equal to 20% of his mortgage interest – £2,800. In total he pays £1,500 Income Tax on his rental income.

As a non-resident, Dennis will pay £9,300 less UK tax on his rental income. With no other UK income, some of his rental income is tax free thanks to his personal allowance and the rest is taxed at just 20%. As a basic-rate taxpayer Dennis is completely unaffected by the mortgage tax relief restriction.

Even though his interest is no longer a tax deductible expense, none of his income is pushed into the 40% tax bracket. The 20% tax he pays on some of his rental income (because his interest costs are not deductible) is completely offset by an identical 20% tax reduction.

Other Issues for Non-Residents

Other UK Income
Non-residents who have other UK income, apart from their rental income, are more likely to be affected by the reduction in interest tax relief.

As a non-resident there is no UK tax payable on salary you receive for doing work outside the UK. However, you could still be subject to UK tax for duties performed in the UK, unless they are "merely incidental" to your overseas job.

If you retire abroad you will probably receive a UK pension. Under the terms of many of the UK's double tax treaties, only the country where you live can tax your pension. Thus many retirees do not pay any UK tax on their UK pensions. Government pensions are an exception. Tax is usually only payable in the UK, with no tax payable overseas. Note that every double tax agreement has different terms, so you will need to do a bit of research before you emigrate.

Some countries don't have a double tax agreement with the UK and in these cases your pension will remain taxable in the UK.

Personal Allowance
Not all non-residents are entitled to a personal allowance to set against their UK rental (or other) income. The normal personal allowance (£12,500 this year) is currently available to:

- British nationals resident abroad
- Nationals of states within the European Economic Area
- Crown servants
- Residents of the Isle of Man
- Residents of the Channel Islands
- Residents of countries which have a suitable double taxation agreement with the UK

Capital Gains Tax

Emigration may not only help you reduce your UK Income Tax, it may also help you pay less Capital Gains Tax.

Non-residents are no longer completely exempt from Capital Gains Tax when they sell UK residential property. However, only gains that have arisen since 6th April 2015 are taxable.

Gains that arose before this date are completely free from UK tax, providing you remain non-resident for more than five years.

Overseas Tax

Your UK rental income may also be taxable in the country where you are now resident for tax purposes. If this is the case, any UK tax you pay will probably be allowed as a credit against your overseas tax bill.

Some countries are more generous than others and offer concessions to new residents such as a tax exemption for their overseas (i.e. UK) income. Australia is one such country.

Mortgage Issues

Becoming non-resident could affect your ability to take out new mortgages or remortgage existing properties because only a small proportion of buy-to-let lenders currently offer their products to expats.

For example, if your existing fixed-rate deals come to an end while you are non-resident, you could be stuck paying the lender's standard variable rate (or other "revert to" rate) unless you can find new fixed-rate deals from another lender who is willing to deal with expats.

Chapter 21

Investing in Different Types of Property

As explained in Chapter 3, the interest relief restrictions do not apply to funds borrowed for investment in non-residential property, or in qualifying furnished holiday lettings.

As far as future investments are concerned, it would be a relatively simple matter for an investor to change their strategy and begin building a portfolio of either commercial property (shops, offices, pubs, restaurants, etc) or furnished holiday lettings.

Managing these investments does require a different 'skill set', however, and this is something a residential landlord should bear in mind.

Furthermore, a property can only qualify as a furnished holiday let if certain strict criteria are met (see the Taxcafe.co.uk guide *'How to Save Property Tax'* for details).

In any case, we're not convinced many residential landlords have a burning desire to start investing in commercial property or furnished holiday lettings – most lay empty throughout the coronavirus lockdown and that can't have inspired confidence in those sectors.

Converting Existing Property

In some cases, it may be possible to convert existing property to either commercial use or to a furnished holiday let.

A city-centre ground floor flat might be suitable for converting into a cafe; the upper storeys of the same building might be suitable for furnished holiday letting; or the whole property might make a good office building.

Rural properties may often lend themselves to furnished holiday letting too.

All of this depends on the type of property, its location, and on obtaining the necessary permission for 'change of use'. Not all properties will be suitable, but it may be worth considering the idea in some cases.

Better Borrowing

In some cases, there may be scope to effectively arrange your borrowings so that more of them relate to non-residential property or furnished holiday lettings.

The simple idea of mortgaging a commercial property or furnished holiday let and using the funds to pay off the mortgage on a residential property will not work, however, as the new borrowings will clearly have been invested in residential property.

However, let us suppose that you have £100,000 of available cash (e.g. from the sale of a rental property) and you use this to pay off the mortgage on a residential property.

Then, a year or two later, you might invest in a commercial property or a furnished holiday let. You could borrow against the new property, or indeed any other property, use the funds for your investment and retain full tax relief on the interest arising (plus the loan arrangement fees and other associated costs).

If, instead, you had simply used the £100,000 of cash to purchase your new investment, you would have been left with a mortgage on a residential property with interest relief restricted to basic rate only.

Overseas Property

Interest on borrowings used to finance purchases of overseas residential property is subject to the same restrictions as for purchases of UK residential property.

There are therefore only two ways in which investing in overseas residential property might help with your interest relief restriction:

i)   Property in the European Economic Area that qualifies as a furnished holiday let is exempt from the interest relief restriction

ii) If you were to emigrate and become non-UK resident at some stage in the future, you would cease to be subject to UK Income Tax on rental income from overseas property

When investing in overseas property, it is essential to bear in mind that you may be subject to tax in the country in which the property is located. Those who emigrate will also generally be subject to tax in the country in which they are resident for tax purposes.

Chapter 22

Alternative Investment Structures

Higher-rate taxpayers who wish to make new property investments may wish to consider using alternative investment structures in order to avoid the problem of being taxed on 'profits' they will not receive if they were to use the traditional buy-to-let mortgage model.

Shared Equity

Rather than borrow the funds required to make a purchase, it may be possible to enter into a shared equity arrangement whereby the property is effectively shared with another party.

Example
Morgan is a higher rate taxpayer. She wishes to purchase a residential property valued at £100,000 but has only £75,000 available to invest. The property will produce a rental profit (after all expenses except interest) of £5,000. If Morgan borrows the additional £25,000 she needs, she will incur an annual interest cost of £1,000. Her net tax liability on the income from the property would be £1,800 (£5,000 x 40% less £1,000 x 20%), leaving her with after tax income of £2,200.

Instead, Morgan enters into a shared equity arrangement whereby she purchases a 75% share of the property for £75,000 and another party acquires a 25% share. It is agreed that Morgan will receive 80% of the net rental profit: her increased share reflecting the fact she will be managing the property.

Morgan now has a rental profit of £4,000 (£5,000 x 80%), a tax liability of £1,600 (£4,000 x 40%), and is left with after tax income of £2,400: i.e. £200 more than if she had taken out a mortgage.

This strategy would be even more worthwhile for a landlord with a marginal tax rate greater than 40%.

The downside is that Morgan will be losing out on 25% of the property's capital growth.

Syndicates

Another way to invest in property without borrowing is to invest via a syndicate.

For example, four additional rate taxpayers could each invest £50,000 in a residential rental property and would each receive rental profits of, say, £2,500, leaving each of them with after tax income of £1,375 (after tax at 45%).

If, instead, each had gone out and borrowed £150,000 at 4% and bought their own £200,000 property, then each would receive rental profits of £10,000 taxed at 45% (£4,500), and pay interest of £6,000, which would attract tax relief at just 20% (£1,200). Each investor's after tax income would then be just £700 (£10,000 - £4,500 - £6,000 + £1,200).

Using the syndicate almost doubles each investor's return!

The downside, once again, is that each investor is enjoying less capital growth: only a quarter share in this case in fact.

Note
Using the same figures for higher-rate taxpayers with a marginal tax rate of 40% produces after tax income of £1,500 each using a syndicate compared with £1,200 using a buy-to-let mortgage. Not quite as beneficial, but still better overall (from an income perspective).

Chapter 23

Transferring Property to Your Spouse or Partner

Making sure properties are owned by the spouse or partner with the lowest tax rate is a well-known tax saving technique.

This strategy may become even more popular now the restriction to tax relief on mortgage interest has been fully phased in.

Example
Shakeel is a higher-rate taxpayer with self-employment income of £50,000 from a small shop. He also owns a flat that generates net rental income of £10,000 and pays £5,000 interest on his buy-to-let mortgage.

With none of his interest tax deductible his taxable rental profit will be £10,000. He'll pay 40% tax (£4,000) but will also be entitled to a tax reduction equal to 20% of his mortgage interest (£1,000), so his total tax bill on the rental income will be £3,000.

Shakeel's wife Nazreen earns a salary of £20,000 and is a basic-rate taxpayer. If Nazreen owns the property she'll pay 20% tax on the £10,000 rental profit (£2,000) but will also be entitled to a 20% tax reduction (£1,000), so her total tax bill on the rental income will be £1,000 – exactly what she would pay if her interest was fully tax deductible. As a basic-rate taxpayer she is completely unaffected by the change to interest tax relief.

The couple will save £2,000 if Nazreen owns the property.

Who Can Save Tax?

Tax savings are typically possible when the transferor is a higher-rate taxpayer and the transferee is a basic-rate taxpayer (and remains a basic-rate taxpayer after the transfer).

Additional savings may be possible if the household receives child benefit and, thanks to the transfer, both spouses end up earning less than £60,000 (and preferably no more than £50,000).

For example, if Shakeel owns the property the couple will effectively lose all their child benefit; if Nazreen owns the property they will lose none of it.

It may also be possible to save more tax by transferring property if one person has now ended up with taxable income over £100,000 (personal allowance withdrawn) or £150,000 (additional-rate tax payable) as a result of the interest relief restrictions.

Future Tax Years

The tax savings enjoyed by transferring property could be short lived.

For example, if a property is transferred to a basic-rate taxpayer and that person eventually becomes a higher-rate taxpayer because they begin to receive pension income, or because their salary or other non-property income grows significantly, the tax savings could then be erased completely.

In other words, when deciding what share of a property to transfer to your spouse or partner you should look ahead to future tax years, rather than focus on the tax savings in a single year alone.

Joint Ownership Basics

When a property is already owned jointly by a couple it may be possible to change the ownership split to produce a better tax outcome but there are some traps to watch out for.

In England and Wales there are two types of joint ownership:

- Joint tenancy
- Tenancy in common

With joint tenancy, each joint owner is treated as having an equal share of the property and the income is split 50:50 (subject to the further points below regarding unmarried joint owners).

With tenancy in common, the shares in the property do not have to be equal. A tenancy in common therefore provides far more scope for tax planning.

In Scotland the most common form of joint ownership is *Pro Indivisio*, which is much the same as a tenancy in common.

It's important to point out that a joint tenancy can be changed to a tenancy in common.

Income Tax Elections

Where a property is held jointly by a married couple, the default Income Tax treatment is a 50:50 split, even if the property is owned in unequal shares.

If you want to be taxed according to your actual beneficial ownership of the property you have to make an election using Form 17 from HMRC. On this form you state the proportions in which the property is owned and this determines how the rental profits are divided for Income Tax purposes.

Such an election will be permanently binding unless the ownership split changes.

Unmarried Couples

A property (or a share in a property) can be transferred from one legally married spouse to the other without any Capital Gains Tax charge arising.

With unmarried couples, a transfer from one partner to the other, or into joint names, can result in a Capital Gains Tax charge. The property, or share in the property, which is transferred is taxed as if it had been sold for its market value.

For this reason, it is preferable to get the ownership split right when the property is acquired.

Having said this, joint owners who are not married can agree to split the rental income in a different proportion to their legal ownership of the property.

Hence, for example, an unmarried couple who own a property in equal shares could agree that one person is entitled to 75% of the rental income and the other is entitled to 25%.

It is important to have the income split properly documented in a signed and dated profit-sharing agreement before the start of the tax year, and it is probably advisable to have the income paid into separate bank accounts.

Stamp Duty Land Tax (SDLT)

Purchases or transfers of property located in England or Northern Ireland are subject to Stamp Duty Land Tax.

Stamp Duty Land Tax may be incurred when a mortgaged property is transferred to a spouse. The potential one-off tax payment will have to be weighed against the potential annual Income Tax saving the couple hopes to achieve.

Even if your spouse doesn't pay you anything for their share of the property, SDLT may be payable if they take on part of the mortgage or other debt over the property. This is because any debt, or share of debt, which the transferee takes on is effectively deemed to form purchase consideration for SDLT purposes. However, due to the temporary reduction in Stamp Duty Land Tax rates currently applying (see further below), now could be a good time to make the transfer.

The basic rates of SDLT on residential property are normally:

Up to £125,000	Nil
£125,000 to £250,000	2%
£250,000 to £925,000	5%
£925,000 to £1.5m	10%
Over £1.5m	12%

However, for the period from 8th July 2020 to 31st March 2021 (inclusive), the rates have been reduced, as follows:

Up to £500,000	Nil
£500,000 to £925,000	5%
£925,000 to £1.5m	10%
Over £1.5m	12%

An extra 3% surcharge is payable on additional residential properties such as buy-to-let properties and second homes. Initially this surcharge generally applied to transfers of residential rental property between spouses, based on the amount of mortgage debt effectively taken over by the transferee.

However, since 22nd November 2017, transfers between spouses have been exempt from the additional 3% surcharge. The couple must be living together at the time of the transfer for the exemption to apply.

Where the exemption applies, Stamp Duty Land Tax remains payable on the amount of debt taken over by the transferee, but only at the normal 'basic' rates set out above. For example, where a 50% share of a property with a £400,000 mortgage is transferred, the Stamp Duty Land Tax bill would normally be £1,500:

$$£125,000 \text{ x } 0\% + £75,000 \text{ x } 2\% = £1,500$$

However, the good news is that, until 31st March 2021, while the temporary reduction in Stamp Duty Land Tax rates applies, there would be no charge on such a transfer.

In fact, a 50% share of a property with a mortgage of anything up to *£1 million* can currently be transferred to a spouse with no Stamp Duty Land Tax liability. (From 1st April 2021, there will again be a charge on a transfer of a 50% share in any property with a mortgage over £250,000.)

Transfers of rental property between unmarried partners will generally continue to be subject to the additional 3% surcharge (as well as Capital Gains Tax – as explained above). However, the surcharge only applies if the total purchase consideration is £40,000 or more. For purchases at less than £40,000, no Stamp Duty Land Tax is payable. Hence, an unmarried partner could take on a 50% joint share in a property with a mortgage of up to £79,999 without incurring any Stamp Duty Land Tax liability.

If a 50% share of a property with a £200,000 mortgage is transferred from one unmarried partner to another, the Stamp Duty Land Tax charge would be £3,000 (£100,000 x 3%). Capital Gains Tax might also arise on the transfer.

Property in Scotland

Purchases or transfers of property located in Scotland are subject to Land and Buildings Transaction Tax (LBTT). The basic rates on residential property are as follows:

£0 to £145,000	0%
£145,000 to £250,000	2%
£250,000 to £325,000	5%
£325,000 to £750,000	10%
Over £750,000	12%

However, the rate on the £145,000 to £250,000 band is to be temporarily reduced to 0%. At the time of writing, we are told this reduction will commence 'as soon as possible' and will apply until 31st March 2021.

A similar additional surcharge, known as the 'Additional Dwelling Supplement', applies to purchases or transfers of residential rental property, even if the person acquiring the property has no other interest in residential property.

The Additional Dwelling Supplement was increased from 3% to 4% on 25th January 2019.

As with Stamp Duty Land Tax, any debt, or share of debt, taken on by the transferee is deemed to form purchase consideration for Land and Buildings Transaction Tax purposes.

Unlike the Stamp Duty Land Tax surcharge, there is no exemption from the Additional Dwelling Supplement for transfers between spouses. Hence, when a residential rental property located in Scotland is transferred between spouses, the transferee is in the same position as any other transferee and Additional Dwelling Supplement will be payable whenever the mortgage, or share of mortgage, taken over, is £40,000 or more.

Apart from the points set out above, LBTT operates in a broadly similar way to SDLT, although there are some important variations, so professional advice is essential when purchasing or transferring property in Scotland.

At the time of writing, we do not know when the temporary reduction in the LBTT rate referred to above will come into force. The maximum potential saving involved is £2,100 so, for a transfer to a spouse or partner, it may be worth holding off making the transfer for a short while in some cases, until the reduction comes into force.

Property in Wales

SDLT ceased to apply to property located in Wales from 1st April 2018. It has been replaced by Land Transaction Tax (LTT), the first devolved tax for Wales.

The basic rates of LTT on residential property are as follows:

£0 to £180,000	0%
£180,000 to £250,000	3.5%
£250,000 to £400,000	5%
£400,000 to £750,000	7.5%
£750,000 to £1.5 million	10%
Over £1.5 million	12%

As usual, there is an additional 3% surcharge on most purchases or transfers of residential rental property.

LTT also operates in a broadly similar way to SDLT but again, there are some important variations, so professional advice is essential when purchasing or transferring property in Wales.

At the time of writing, there has not been any announcement regarding any temporary reduction in LTT rates to mirror those for SDLT and LBTT, although many are calling for this to happen. Hence, it may be worth just holding off on any transfers of property located in Wales for a short period, or taking professional advice on this point before you go ahead with the transfer.

Avoiding SDLT, LBTT, and LTT

As far as SDLT is concerned, the simplest way to avoid paying this tax on a transfer to a <u>spouse</u>, in most cases, will be to make sure the transfer is completed by 31st March 2021: no charge will arise where the total of any actual or deemed consideration (such as taking on a share of mortgage debt) does not exceed £500,000.

In other cases, the simplest way to avoid paying these taxes when a property is transferred to a spouse or partner is to pay off or reduce the mortgage first (for example, by remortgaging another property).

Once the transfer is complete it may be possible to take out a fresh mortgage against the transferred property.

Some landlords may, however, find it difficult to do this sort of juggling act.

Mortgage Issues

One of the biggest potential stumbling blocks when transferring property to your spouse used to be getting permission from the lender, especially if the spouse had only a modest earned income.

However, as the tax rules for buy-to-let properties get increasingly complicated making sure any changes in property ownership don't have unintended consequences is an increasing risk.

According to Ray Boulger, senior mortgage technical manager at mortgage broker John Charcol, if a property is transferred outright from one spouse to another the transferee will have to satisfy the lender's criteria and it would be treated as a new application, thus incurring mortgage fees as well as legal costs.

Most lenders also require the borrower to have a minimum earned income, typically £25,000.

A much better solution, he says, which would allow the mortgage to remain unchanged and incur relatively low legal and mortgage costs, may be to effect a "transfer of equity". This is the process whereby someone is added to the title deeds and requires permission from the lender.

According to Mr Boulger: "Assuming the property is 100% owned, it could be transferred into joint ownership on a tenants-in-common basis with, for example, the spouse or partner owning 99% and the original owner 1%."

This arrangement is also suitable for purchases and another option for purchases is now offered by several lenders. This is known as sole proprietor, joint borrower; the property is purchased in the sole name of the non or low taxpayer but the lender offers a mortgage in joint names with the spouse/partner, as a result of which even someone with no income could use a mortgage to buy a property.

With both options the mortgage would be on a joint and several liability basis and in the first case the new joint owner would be added to the mortgage with relatively little formality.

Transferring other Assets to Your Spouse

Where transferring a property to your spouse is not possible or is not practical for some reason, it's important to remember that a similar result can often be achieved by transferring other income producing assets. For example, if you own a company it may be possible to transfer shares to your spouse so that he or she can receive dividends taxed at a lower rate than you.

Splitting Income in the Current Climate

As mentioned earlier, tax savings are typically achieved when the original owner of the property is a higher-rate taxpayer and the person to whom it's transferred is a basic-rate taxpayer.

This year, of course, many taxpayers' incomes have fallen dramatically. In some cases the tax savings that could previously have been achieved by transferring property will have disappeared – for example, the couple may both be basic-rate taxpayers this year.

This state of affairs may last for more than one tax year.

For some couples there may, therefore, be no immediate rush to make property transfers to avoid the mortgage tax change and save income tax.

This takes us back to the point made previously: When deciding what share of a property to transfer to your spouse or partner you should look ahead to future tax years, rather than focus on the tax savings in a single year alone.

Chapter 24

Using a Company to Save Tax

Introduction

Interest in using companies to invest in residential property surged after the announcement that tax relief on finance costs would be reduced for *individual* landlords. Companies are exempt from the tax change.

It has not been good news all round for company owners on the tax front, however. Initially, the Government also considered an exemption from the 3% Stamp Duty Land Tax surcharge for companies making "significant" investments in residential property. In the end it was decided that all investors will pay the same Stamp Duty Land Tax. The higher rates apply to all companies purchasing residential property (including their first purchase of a residential property).

Then in 2016 Income Tax on dividends was increased significantly and in the March 2020 Budget the Government confirmed that the Corporation Tax rate would not be cut from 19% to 17% in April 2020. We now expect the cut to be shelved indefinitely.

In this chapter, we will provide an overview of the tax benefits and drawbacks of using a company to invest in property but, for a more complete discussion of the issues, we recommend reading the Taxcafe.co.uk guide *'Using a Property Company to Save Tax'*.

Interest Relief in Companies

The restriction to residential landlords' interest relief specifically does not apply to companies (unless the company is acting in a fiduciary or representative capacity as a nominee, etc).

However, in the March 2016 Budget a new restriction on the amount of interest relief that companies can claim was announced. It is aimed principally at multinational groups that use interest payments to shift profits out of the UK but theoretically applies to all companies.

From 1st April 2017 interest relief has been capped at 30% of taxable earnings before interest, tax, depreciation and amortisation (EBITDA) in the UK.

But most small company owners will be unaffected because the restriction generally only applies to companies whose annual interest costs exceed £2 million.

Even for those with annual interest costs in excess of £2 million, there is an alternative option to claim interest relief on an amount equal to the average proportion of net interest to EBITDA for the worldwide group.

Hence, UK companies with no associated companies overseas will also be unaffected.

Thus the new rules will not affect the vast majority of privately owned companies. However, that is not to say that the Government could not, at some point in the future, introduce other restrictions specifically targeted at privately owned property companies investing in residential property.

Here we would classify the risk as 'medium'. Readers must bear these risks in mind but, for the remainder of this chapter, we will assume that the current regime for interest relief in companies continues to apply.

Tax on Rental Income

Companies that own rental property pay just 19% Corporation Tax on all their rental profits whereas individual landlords who are higher-rate taxpayers pay 40% Income Tax.

Individual landlords may also suffer other "penalties" including the High Income Child Benefit Charge (taxable income over £50,000), withdrawal of their personal allowance (taxable income over £100,000) and the 45% additional rate of tax (taxable income over £150,000).

Property investors with large taxable rental profits may therefore end up with significantly more *after-tax* income if the properties are held inside a company. This extra income can then be reinvested to grow the business.

Example

Benny works full-time and also owns a fairly large residential property business. In 2020/21 he earns a salary of £50,000 from his separate job. His property business has net rental income of £125,000 after deducting all costs except mortgage interest which comes to £40,000 per year. So his true rental profit is £85,000.

If Benny owns the properties <u>personally</u> (i.e. outside a company) he'll have a taxable rental profit of £125,000 and none of his interest will be tax deductible. His total taxable income will be £175,000.

With this much taxable income he will lose his Income Tax personal allowance and will pay Income Tax at 20% on the first £37,500 (the basic-rate band in 2020/21), 40% on the next £112,500, and 45% on the final £25,000. This will result in a tax liability of £63,750.

He will also be entitled to a tax reduction equal to 20% of his finance costs – £8,000 – so his final Income Tax bill will come to £55,750.

If instead the properties were held inside a <u>company</u> all the interest would be tax deductible and the taxable rental profit would be £85,000. Corporation tax at 19% would come to £16,150.

Benny would also pay Income Tax on his salary. The first £12,500 would be tax free (the personal allowance in 2020/21) and the remaining £37,500 would be taxed at 20%, producing a total Income Tax bill of £7,500.

In summary, Benny's total annual tax bill will be £32,100 lower if he uses a company to hold his properties. This money can be rolled up inside the company and used to invest in additional properties.

Profit Extraction = Additional Tax

Clearly if Benny reinvests all his rental profits he will be significantly better off using a company, at least when it comes to saving *Income Tax* (we will look at Capital Gains Tax later).

But what if he needs to extract some or all of the money, for example to pay his household bills? In that case an additional Income Tax charge will typically arise.

For the average company owner, a dividend is the most tax efficient way to take a significant amount of money out of the company on an ongoing basis.

However, a small salary is often the first port of call. A salary will provide a Corporation Tax saving for the company itself (because it's a tax deductible expense) and, providing the salary is kept small enough, there will be little or no national insurance payable either.

A salary equal to the personal allowance (£12,500 this year) is often optimal where the company owner has no income from other sources, and the company has very few (but at least one) other paid employees.

Where the company owner has no income from other sources, and is the company's only employee (as director), or the company has many employees, a salary no higher than the primary National Insurance threshold (£9,500 this year) will generally be most tax efficient.

Such a salary (i.e. £9,500 this year) will also generally be most tax efficient where the company owner **does** have income from other sources, but the company has very few (but at least one) other paid employees.

In other cases, a salary no higher than the secondary National Insurance threshold (£8,788 this year) will generally be most tax efficient.

A second director (e.g. the owner's spouse or partner) may count as another employee for these purposes, provided they are paid a salary in excess of the secondary National Insurance threshold (£8,788 this year).

Dividends are paid out of a company's *after-tax profits*, i.e. after Corporation Tax has already been paid. Once a small salary has been taken, dividends are generally most tax efficient.

For full details of the most tax efficient ways to extract profits from a company, see the Taxcafe.co.uk guide *'Salary versus Dividends'*.

Since 2016, new tax rates have applied to dividend income. Dividend tax credits have been abolished, so it is no longer necessary to gross up your dividends to calculate your tax. All tax calculations now work with the amount of dividend actually paid.

The bad news is that the current tax rates for dividends are 7.5% higher than the old rates. The first £2,000 of dividend income is, however, tax free thanks to the "dividend allowance".

For those receiving dividends in excess of the dividend allowance, the following Income Tax rates apply (the previous effective rates on cash dividends are included for comparison):

	Old rates	**Current rates**
Basic-rate taxpayers	0%	7.5%
Higher-rate taxpayers	25%	32.5%
Additional-rate taxpayers	30.6%	38.1%

Example continued

If Benny uses a company it will pay £16,150 Corporation Tax on its £85,000 rental profit, leaving a £68,850 after-tax profit. Let's say Benny extracts the whole £68,850 as a dividend. Added to his £50,000 salary this gives him total taxable income of £118,850.

With this much income his personal allowance will be reduced from £12,500 to £3,075 so only this much of his salary income will be tax free. The next £37,500 of his salary will be taxed at 20% and the final £9,425 will be taxed at 40%.

Turning to his dividend income, the first £2,000 will be tax free thanks to the dividend allowance and the remaining £66,850 will be taxed at 32.5%.

Benny's total Income Tax bill will be £32,996, which means he'll be left with an after-tax income of £85,854:

£50,000 salary + £68,850 dividend - £32,996 tax = £85,854

How does this compare with owning the properties personally? As we know from the previous example, Benny would face an Income Tax bill of £55,750, which means he would be left with an after-tax income of £79,250:

£50,000 salary + £85,000 rental profit - £55,750 tax = £79,250

Benny is still better off to the tune of £6,604 by using a company.

(We have ignored the National Insurance on Benny's salary throughout this example for the sake of illustration. This has no effect on his final overall saving as his National Insurance cost remains the same under both scenarios.)

Note that, for the reasons explained earlier, taking a small second salary from his property company equal to the National Insurance secondary threshold (£8,788 this year) would have left Benny slightly better off. For detailed calculations of the impact of a small salary on a company owner's overall tax savings, see the Taxcafe.co.uk guide *'Salary versus Dividends'*.

Not all personal versus company calculations will produce such a favourable outcome for the company investor so it is essential to do your own number crunching to determine the potential Income Tax savings.

Nevertheless it is worth mentioning that one of the advantages of being a company owner is that you have complete control over how much income you withdraw each year. This gives you significant control over your personal Income Tax bill.

Property investors who own their properties personally must pay Income Tax each year on ALL the profits of the business. By contrast, company owners only pay Income Tax on the money they actually withdraw from the company.

This often allows them to stay below key Income Tax thresholds that could result in a higher Income Tax bill.

For instance, Benny in the above example could have taken a dividend of just £50,000 instead of £68,850. This would have kept his taxable income at £100,000, allowing him to hold onto all of his Income Tax personal allowance.

Tax on Capital Gains

If you sell a rental property that you own *personally* you will, of course, be subject to Capital Gains Tax. For residential property sales, the taxable gain will typically be taxed at 28% if you are a higher-rate taxpayer (18% to the extent your basic-rate band is not used up by your income).

These rates have been reduced to 20% and 10% respectively for sales of most other assets, including commercial property, but the old, higher rates remain in force for residential property.

Very few property investors qualify for entrepreneurs relief, which allows up to £1 million of capital gains to be taxed at just 10% (typically this relief is reserved for business owners who sell their trading business, although it can sometimes also apply to furnished holiday lets).

Companies that sell rental properties pay Corporation Tax on their capital gains at the rate of 19%. Even though the rate has not been reduced to 17% (the Government's previous, but unfulfilled, promise), this is still lower than the 28% paid by individuals who are higher-rate taxpayers and sell residential property.

Individuals and companies also qualify for different capital gains reliefs.

Established companies may enjoy some indexation relief, which means they do not have to pay tax on some of the increase in the property's price that was simply caused by inflation.

However, indexation relief has been frozen with effect from 31st December 2017.

Take a company that bought a property in January 2010 and sells it in December 2025. Indexation relief will be available from January 2010 to December 2017, but not from January 2018 to December 2025.

This is a blow to company owners because indexation relief has previously taken a large chunk of company capital gains out of the tax net.

Individuals, on the other hand, receive a Capital Gains Tax annual exemption, which currently exempts the first £12,300 of their gains from tax (£24,600 if the property is owned by a couple).

Companies also cannot benefit from the principal private residence exemption and private letting relief which can reduce the Capital Gains Tax payable by individual investors who have used a property as their main residence at some point. However, both of these reliefs have been restricted since 6th April 2020.

In summary, companies will often pay less tax on capital gains arising on regular residential rental properties than higher-rate taxpayer individuals. This is beneficial when properties are being sold occasionally with the proceeds reinvested in new ones.

However, the comparison between personal and company ownership becomes much more complex when the investor wants to wind up the property business and extract money from the company.

Extracting Capital Gains from a Company

Company investors who want to sell up essentially have three main choices:

- Sell the company (i.e. sell the shares)
- Company sells the properties and pays dividends
- Company sells the properties and is wound up

Note that any loans you have made to the company can always be repaid to you tax free and it generally makes sense to withdraw these funds first before proceeding with any other steps.

Selling the Company

A company owner who sells their shares (rather than getting the company to sell the underlying properties) is subject to Capital Gains Tax at the new reduced rates. In other words, you will pay 20% tax if you are a higher-rate taxpayer, reduced to 10% to the extent that your income does not use up your basic-rate band. You will also be entitled to the annual Capital Gains Tax exemption.

Thus if a company owner sells their shares they could end up paying less Capital Gains Tax than an individual investor who owns an identical property portfolio and has to pay up to 28% tax (although the company investor would hopefully have a bigger portfolio if they've been reinvesting their less heavily taxed rental profits).

In practice, however, it may be more difficult to sell the company than the properties themselves. Many potential buyers will shy away from buying a company because they fear that doing so may expose them to all of the company's liabilities, some of which may not be known when the company is acquired.

Furthermore, a sensible purchaser would expect to discount the value of the company's shares to take account of the Corporation Tax which would be payable on the capital gains arising within the company if it were to sell the properties it holds.

Selling the Properties and Paying Dividends

An alternative would be to get the company to sell the properties and pay out the after-tax profits as dividends.

Paying dividends will result in double tax. The company will pay Corporation Tax on the capital gains and the company owner will pay Income Tax on the after-tax profits paid out as dividends. This could result in a total of just over £45 tax being paid on every £100 of taxable capital gain – an overall tax rate of just over 45%:

£100 x 19% Corporation Tax + £81 x 32.5% Income Tax = £45.325

This calculation ignores the dividend allowance, which will exempt the first £2,000 of dividend income you receive from tax. It also assumes the company owner is a higher-rate taxpayer and is subject to 32.5% Income Tax on all dividend payments.

If the dividends take the company owner's income over the £100,000 threshold they will also start to lose their Income Tax personal allowance and if they take the owner's income over £150,000 they will pay 38.1% tax on some of their income.

It may be possible to spread the dividend payments over several tax years to avoid these two "tax penalties".

Although 45% is a lot higher than the 28% maximum Capital Gains Tax rate paid by individual investors, it is possible that a company will have enjoyed significantly higher after-tax rental profits because it will have paid Corporation Tax on its rental income instead of Income Tax.

If those profits have been reinvested to build a significantly bigger property portfolio, it is possible this could more than compensate for the higher tax rate at the end.

Company owners may also be able to pay just 7.5% Income Tax if they are basic-rate taxpayers when they withdraw dividends.

This could result in a total of around £25 tax being paid on every £100 of taxable capital gain, i.e. an effective overall tax rate of around 25%:

$$£100 \times 19\% \text{ Corporation Tax} + £81 \times 7.5\% = £25.075$$

Extracting dividends as a basic-rate taxpayer may be possible if the dividends are only paid out when the company owner has very little income from other sources (e.g. after retiring) and can spread the dividend payments over several tax years (to utilise several years' worth of basic-rate band).

The process could also be speeded up if the company is owned by a couple so that two basic-rate bands can be used each year.

Of course property investors who own residential properties personally can adopt a similar tactic to reduce their Capital Gains Tax rate from 28% to 18%. They can spread their property sales over several years so that multiple basic-rate bands and Capital Gains Tax annual exemptions can be utilised.

So again, the benefit of using a company will probably boil down to whether the investor has been able to use the low Corporation Tax rate to build a much bigger portfolio inside the company.

Selling the Properties and Winding Up the Company

Under this scenario the company sells the properties and pays out the after-tax profits as a *capital distribution*.

A capital distribution will also result in a double tax charge. The company will pay Corporation Tax on the property capital gains and the company owner will pay Capital Gains Tax on the after-tax profits paid out.

Winding up a company can be a very expensive process in terms of fees, especially if the company still has assets and liabilities, or has recently been in active business.

In simple cases, where the company has been inactive for some time and perhaps only holds cash, you can, alternatively, apply to have it struck off. This is a simpler, cheaper and quicker process.

However, striking off (or 'dissolving') a company has some important legal implications. Furthermore, any sums in excess of £25,000 (in total) which are distributed to shareholders **must** be taxed as income.

For these reasons, it is usually sensible to go for a winding up (a 'members' voluntary liquidation', to give it its formal name) in all but the very simplest cases, so we will assume that is the case for the remainder of this chapter (unless specifically stated to the contrary). Either way though, it is wise to seek professional advice before you act!

Distribution Problems

New rules applying since 2016 mean that, in some cases, the profits distributed on a winding up may have to be treated as dividends rather than capital gains.

These new rules apply where:

- The individual holds at least 5% of the share capital and voting rights immediately before the winding up and the company is a close company at some point in the two years before the winding up,

- Within two years of the distribution the company owner carries on the same or a similar trade or activity to the company being wound up, and

- It is reasonable to assume that the main purpose, or one of the main purposes, of the winding up is to achieve a reduction in Income Tax, OR
The winding up forms part of arrangements, one of the main purposes of which is to achieve a reduction in Income Tax

At present, based on the view taken by some expert commentators, it seems likely these new rules could apply when many property companies are wound up. This is because:

i)   The vast majority of private companies are close companies (at least 11 unconnected shareholders are needed in order to avoid this).

ii)   The owner of a property investment company would meet the second test above if they, any other company they own, their spouse, or any other close relative, continues to invest in property after the winding up.

iii)   Some expert commentators believe HMRC will interpret the third test very broadly: in particular, they fear that declining to pay surplus funds out as dividends prior to the winding up could, in itself, be enough to be regarded as an 'arrangement' to reduce Income Tax.

We are not entirely convinced that the third test should be interpreted quite so broadly. Furthermore, it is not for HM Revenue and Customs to decide the matter: that power, as in all tax disputes, ultimately lies with the courts.

Nevertheless, even if one takes a more optimistic stance on the third test, the new rules still cast a significant doubt over the treatment of profits distributed on a winding up.

Hence, unless you can make sure your company is owned by at least 11 unconnected people, or can ensure that neither you nor any of your close relatives will invest in property (directly, through a company, or through some other type of entity) after you wind up your company, it seems wisest at this point to assume that the profits distributed to you will have to be treated as a dividend.

That being so, it may make sense to pay actual dividends over the course of a few tax years (as explained above) rather than making a single large distribution when you wind up the company.

One single large distribution may lead to a loss of your personal allowance (with an extra tax cost of between £4,063 and £5,625 at current rates), plus additional rate tax on some of the funds distributed (where these take your total taxable income for the year over £150,000).

Where additional rate tax applies, this would result in a total of around £50 tax being paid on every £100 of taxable capital gain; i.e. an effective overall tax rate of around 50%:

£100 x 19% Corporation Tax + £81 x 38.1% = £49.86

Remember, adopting a phased approach to the withdrawal of profits from your company should enable you to enjoy the overall effective rates of around 45% or even 25% described above.

A More Optimistic View

At this stage, we would advocate planning on the basis that the new rules regarding profits distributed on a winding up will apply when you come to sell your portfolio. Hence the previous strategy of paying sale proceeds out as dividends will be preferable and you should plan accordingly.

However, it may be that by the time you do come to sell your portfolio, the third test might have been examined in court and may not be interpreted quite so widely as some people are currently suggesting. Or you may have managed to ensure you do not meet one of the first two tests (all three tests must be met for you to be caught by the new rules).

Either way, you may by then be in a position to wind up your company without having the profits distributed on the winding up taxed as a dividend.

If that is the case then you would be able to get your hands on all the money in a single tax year without being subject to the extortionate Income Tax rates that apply when large dividend payments are received.

As with dividends, however, this approach will still result in a double tax charge. When the company sells the properties it will pay Corporation Tax on its capital gains and you will pay Capital Gains Tax on the proceeds distributed.

Remember, as explained above, any loans you have made to the company should generally be repaid to you first and these sums will be tax free.

When calculating your Capital Gains Tax, you can also deduct the amount you originally invested in the company as share capital. We generally advise investors to keep their company's share capital to a small nominal sum, such as £100, and to make any further investments in the company by way of loan. Loans can easily be repaid whenever the company has the funds to do so, whereas share capital can only be repaid under certain limited circumstances (including a winding up, or having the company struck off – subject to the issues covered above). For this reason, loans are generally preferable, with just a small nominal sum being invested as share capital.

Either way, the amount which you originally invested will not be subject to Capital Gains Tax. (But see above regarding sums in excess of £25,000 distributed when a company is struck off.)

For example, if the company is left with £250,000 after selling the properties and paying Corporation Tax, the company owner will receive a total of £250,000 on a winding up. If they originally invested, say, £100,000 in the company, their taxable capital gain will be £150,000. (Technically, if the original investment was a loan, the company owner is receiving a loan repayment of £100,000 and a taxable capital distribution of £150,000.)

The double tax charge could result in a total of around £35 tax being paid on every £100 of taxable capital gain, i.e. an effective overall tax rate of around 35%:

£100 x 19% Corporation Tax + £81 x 20% Capital Gains Tax = £35.20

Some of the gain may be taxed at just 10% if your basic-rate band has not been used up by your income, and the Capital Gains Tax annual exemption may also reduce the overall tax bill by up to £2,460 (at current rates).

As usual, any overall benefit that is to be enjoyed by using a company may boil down to whether the investor has been able to use the low Corporation Tax rate to build a much bigger portfolio inside the company. Nonetheless, even when profits have been paid out as dividends in previous years, the cumulative tax savings which the company owner has enjoyed may still outweigh the extra tax arising when the portfolio is eventually sold. Look at Benny in our example above: he saved £6,604 a year even when he took all his company's after tax profits as dividends!

So, does the company pay off in the end? That's a question every property investor has to look at for themselves, based on their own circumstances, their long-term goals, and their own view of future changes to property values, rental yields, interest rates, inflation, and the UK tax regime.

Taxable Capital Gains

For properties purchased after 30th November 2017, the taxable capital gains arising in the company are the total gains on the property and are no longer reduced by indexation relief. New company owners cannot benefit from this relief at all and will thus see no reduction in the effective tax rates set out above.

Future Tax Changes

It's important to make one crucial final point:

Any tax benefit you hope to obtain by using a company could be taken away at the stroke of a pen.

Just as George Osborne practically napalmed landlords before running off to his high paid job in the City, any future Chancellor could drop a similar tax bombshell on property company owners.

Company owners have experienced numerous ups and downs going back to the days when Gordon Brown was Chancellor and beyond. One recent announcement was the freezing of indexation relief, a move which will cost some companies tens of thousands of pounds in Corporation Tax.

Another was the recent decision to cancel the planned cut in Corporation Tax from 19% to 17%.

Throughout 2016 the Orwellian sounding "Office of Tax Simplification" (OTS) investigated a system of "look through" taxation for certain small companies.

A look through system, if made compulsory, would take away the tax benefits of using a company. Under look through taxation, instead of paying Corporation Tax, certain company owners would pay Income Tax and National Insurance on all the profits of the business, just like sole traders and partnerships do.

One of the advantages of using a company is that you can smooth your income and control your Income Tax bill by paying yourself dividends as and when you like. Those who wish to grow their businesses can retain profits inside the company, in which case the only tax payable is 19% Corporation Tax.

Fortunately, the OTS decided not to recommend look through taxation because it would not simplify the tax system and would harm investment. So, hopefully, at least for now, this specific threat has gone away.

Nevertheless the Government seems determined to narrow the gap between the tax paid by regular employees, the self-employed and company owners. Thus we cannot rule out further tax increases at some point in the future.

Furthermore, the recent coronavirus crisis and the huge surge in Government spending to help individuals and businesses through the lockdown may result in steep tax increases in the medium to long-term future.

We don't know what shape any such tax increases will take. For example, there could be increases in Capital Gains Tax and Income Tax (including the tax on company dividends) and any such tax changes could make it more attractive or less attractive to use a company to hold properties.

Chapter 25

Getting Existing Property into a Company

Introduction

Using a company is certainly possible when it comes to making new property acquisitions. The biggest challenge is getting *existing* properties that you already own into a company.

The basic problem with transferring anything into your company is the fact that you and the company are 'connected'. In principle, any transfers of assets between you and the company will be deemed to take place at market value for Capital Gains Tax purposes.

Potentially, therefore, you could face a huge tax bill if you try to transfer existing properties into a company.

Furthermore, most transfers of property to a connected company will also be deemed to take place at market value for Stamp Duty Land Tax purposes. Companies acquiring residential property will be subject to the 3% Stamp Duty Land Tax surcharge mentioned in Chapter 23. The higher SDLT charge applies to every residential property in England or Northern Ireland which is acquired by a company; including both purchases and transfers from the company's owner (see below regarding property in Scotland and Wales).

Multiple dwellings relief can be claimed on any simultaneous transfer of two or more residential dwellings. For a simultaneous transfer of six or more dwellings, the company can also elect to use the non-residential Stamp Duty Land Tax rates.

Non-residential Stamp Duty Land Tax rates are currently as follows:

- First £150,000:   0%
- £150,000 - £250,000:   2%
- Over £250,000:   5%

Example
Michelle has eight residential rental properties worth a total of £1.2m. In November 2020, she transfers them to her own company.

Under basic principles, the company would have to pay SDLT at the higher residential rates (including the 3% surcharge) as follows:

£500,000 x 3% = £15,000
£425,000 x 8% = £34,000
£275,000 x 13% = £35,750
Total: £84,750

Using multiple dwellings relief, however, the Stamp Duty Land Tax would be based on the average value of each property: £150,000; as follows:

£150,000 x 3% = £4,500
Total for eight properties: £36,000 (£4,500 x 8)

Alternatively, the company could elect to pay Stamp Duty Land Tax at non-residential rates, as follows:

£150,000 x 0% = £0
£100,000 x 2% = £2,000
£950,000 x 5% = £47,500
Total: £49,500

Multiple dwellings relief is the best option in Michelle's case, but the non-residential rates will sometimes produce a better result in other cases (where available).

It is important to remember that multiple dwellings relief is based on the number of 'dwellings', not the number of properties.

Hence, for example, if one of Michelle's properties were divided into three self-contained flats, there would be ten dwellings in total and the average value of each 'dwelling' would be just £120,000. At the moment, this would make no difference to her total SDLT bill due to the temporary reduction in SDLT rates but, at other times, and in other cases, it could produce a significant saving.

Despite the heavy SDLT cost on transfers of property to a company, now may be a good time to make those transfers due to the temporary reduction in SDLT rates on residential property that we examined in Chapter 23.

In fact, now could be a good time to make this type of transfer for other reasons too, and we will return to this point later in this chapter.

Property in Scotland

Properties located in Scotland are subject to Land and Buildings Transaction Tax rather than Stamp Duty Land Tax. However, transfers of property to a connected company are again deemed to take place at market value for Land and Buildings Transaction Tax purposes. From 25th January 2019, a 4% surcharge now applies to every residential property in Scotland acquired by a company, either by way of purchase or by way of a transfer from the company's owner. Previously the surcharge was 3%.

Multiple dwellings relief operates in a different way in Scotland: it is generally based on the value of each individual dwelling within the transaction. Note, once again, however, that the relief is based on the value of each 'dwelling' rather than each property.

Multiple dwellings relief cannot reduce the total Land and Buildings Transaction Tax charge to less than 25% of what it would have been without the relief.

A simultaneous transfer of six or more dwellings located in Scotland may again alternatively be taxed at the non-residential rates of Land and Buildings Transaction Tax which, from 25th January 2019, are as follows:

- First £150,000:   0%
- £150,000 - £250,000:   1%
- Over £250,000:   5%

Example

Paul transfers five Scottish residential properties to his own company. One of them is a croft in Assynt worth £30,000, two are houses in Edinburgh worth £275,000 each and the other two are flats in Falkirk worth £90,000 each. Assuming the transfer takes place while the temporary reduction in the LBTT rate applies (see Chapter 23) then, without multiple dwellings relief, the Land and Buildings Transaction Tax payable on the total value of £760,000 would be:

£250,000 x 4% = £10,000
£75,000   x 9% = £6,750
£425,000 x 14% = £59,500
£10,000   x 16% = £1,600
Total: £77,850

Using multiple dwellings relief, however, the Land and Buildings Transaction Tax would be based on the individual value of each property, as follows:

Croft: £30,000 x 0% = £0 x 1 = £0

Falkirk flats: £90,000 x 4% = £3,600 x 2 = £7,200

Edinburgh houses:
£250,000 x 4% = £10,000
£25,000   x 9% = £2,250
Total: £12,250 x 2 = £24,500

Total for all properties: £31,700

This exceeds 25% of the charge without multiple dwellings relief, so this is the charge that will apply.

Example Revisited
Let us now suppose one of Paul's Edinburgh houses has been divided into two self-contained flats. This means he is now transferring six dwellings and the company may elect to use the non-residential Land and Buildings Transaction Tax rates based on the total value of the properties transferred (£760,000):

£150,000 x 0%   = £0
£100,000 x 1%   = £1,000
£510,000 x 5%   = £25,500
Total: £26,500

The charge under multiple dwellings relief would also now be different, as the charge on the two Edinburgh flats (taken together) would now be £11,000 (£275,000 x 4%) instead of £12,250, reducing the overall charge by £1,250, from £31,700 to £30,450.

Nonetheless, the option to use non-residential rates remains preferable.

Hence, once again, the fact the charge is based on the number of 'dwellings' rather than the number of properties has led to a tax saving. Paul would even have saved tax if he had used an additional property worth anything up to £104,000 in order to increase the number of dwellings transferred: although probably not if he had to buy it first.

As explained in Chapter 23, at the time of writing, we do not know when the reduced LBTT rate will come into force. Anyone planning to transfer residential property located in Scotland into a company may therefore wish to hold off for a short period until the reduction is in force. This may save up to £2,100 per property transferred (in Paul's case in our example it will have saved £4,200).

Property in Wales

Stamp Duty Land Tax ceased to apply to property located in Wales from 1st April 2018. It has been replaced by Land Transaction Tax (LTT).

The rates of LTT on residential property were outlined in Chapter 23. Companies acquiring residential property in Wales will also have to pay the additional 3% surcharge.

LTT has its own system of reliefs for multiple acquisitions and is, of course, an extremely new tax, so we recommend taking professional advice if transferring property located in Wales into a company.

As explained in Chapter 23, at the time of writing, there has not, as yet, been any similar announcement regarding any temporary reduction in the rate of LTT to mirror those for SDLT and LBTT, although there are calls for this to happen soon. We would therefore suggest it may be wise to hold off transferring any residential properties located in Wales for a short period until the position is clearer.

Partnerships

A transfer of properties from a partnership business to a company will often enjoy substantial or complete exemption from SDLT.

To obtain the exemption, the company needs to be 'connected' with one or more of the partners. If it is 'connected' with all/both partners, complete exemption is available.

The good news is a company will generally be 'connected' with all/both partners whenever the same individuals own that company.

Hence, **most transfers of partnership property into the partners' own company will be completely exempt from SDLT!**

Furthermore, a company will automatically be 'connected' with all/both partners if all/both of those partners are:

- Spouses or civil partners,
- Siblings, or
- Parents and their adult children

And these individuals also own the company.

Hence, the most obvious example is where a married couple, or a family, have been running a property business as a partnership and they transfer the business to their own company. In many such cases, complete exemption from Stamp Duty Land Tax will be possible.

For other partnerships (including unmarried couples) complete exemption remains available provided all/both partners are individuals acting together to control the company. This will usually be the case, but there will be exceptions.

The exemption applies equally to limited liability partnerships (although these are not usually a good medium through which to invest in property due to some even more restrictive rules on interest relief).

Some people have suggested that a property portfolio which is jointly owned by a married couple, or by any two individuals, is effectively a partnership, even if it has not been formally constituted as one.

Unfortunately, this is not the case, and a formally constituted partnership, which has submitted partnership tax returns, is needed for the exemption to apply.

Others are suggesting it is only necessary to form a partnership for a brief period before transferring property into a company in order to obtain the exemption.

We are not comfortable with this idea as we feel that some of the applicable anti-avoidance legislation could be used to overturn the exemption in such a case.

One thing which is clear, however, is that a transfer of property from a long-term, well established, property partnership run by a married couple, or other qualifying relatives, to a company owned by the same individuals is completely exempt from Stamp Duty Land Tax.

Transfers from other long-term, well established, property partnerships to a company owned by the same individuals will also often be completely exempt.

For property in Scotland held by a partnership, a very similar exemption applies for Land and Buildings Transaction Tax purposes. This again operates to exempt most transfers from a partnership to a company owned by the same individuals.

As previously stated, property in Wales is now subject to Land Transaction Tax, which has its own system of reliefs and exemptions.

Whichever part of the UK the partnership's property is located in, the rules governing this exemption are highly complex, so professional advice is essential.

For further details on the partnership exemption for SDLT (and its equivalents) and on how to formally constitute a partnership, see the Taxcafe.co.uk guide *Using a Property Company to Save Tax*.

Incorporation Relief

As discussed above, the transfer of property into a company could potentially result in significant tax costs.

As far as Capital Gains Tax is concerned, there is an important relief available that may potentially resolve the problem in some cases: incorporation relief.

If a successful claim for incorporation relief is made, the property investor will achieve a tax-free uplift in the base cost of all their properties to current market value.

As residential investment properties would be subject to Capital Gains Tax at 18% or 28% in the transferor's own hands, the uplift in base costs could provide the potential to make massive savings.

Once in the company, properties could generally eventually be sold with a Corporation Tax exposure of just 19% of the future increase in their value.

Incorporation relief should be available whenever any 'business' is transferred to a company wholly or partly in exchange for shares. The problem is there is no statutory definition of what constitutes a business for the purposes of incorporation relief.

Until recently, there was no relevant case law to fall back on either, but the recent case of 'Elisabeth Moyne Ramsay v Revenue and Customs Commissioners' (the 'Ramsay case') has finally shed some light on this issue.

The Twenty Hours a Week Test

Following the Ramsay case, HMRC now accepts that incorporation relief is available where an individual spends an average of at least 20 hours per week on their property business.

What if You Don't Meet the Test?

While HMRC has decided to go along with the idea that 20 hours a week spent on a business means it qualifies for incorporation relief, this is not what the judge in the Ramsay case actually said. Furthermore, even HMRC does not say an investor spending less than 20 hours per week does not qualify, they only say such cases should be 'considered carefully'.

What the judge in the Ramsay case actually said was he accepted Mrs Ramsay had a qualifying business based on all the facts 'taken overall' rather than because of any single factor alone.

Hence, where many of the same factors are present, it is possible the business may still qualify for incorporation relief, even if the owner spends less than 20 hours per week on the business. It is therefore worth us looking at some of the other factors that may have acted in Mrs Ramsay's favour:

- Her property business consisted of a joint interest in a single property divided into ten self-contained flats

- The property had extensive communal areas, as well as a garden, a car park and some garages

- Substantial repairs and maintenance work was carried out on the communal areas, garden, car park and garages

- Mrs Ramsay carried out some of this work personally

- Additional assistance was provided to one elderly tenant

- Prior to the transfer of the property to a company, Mr and Mrs Ramsay carried out some preparatory work regarding a proposed project to refurbish and redevelop the property

- Neither of them had any other occupation during the relevant period

Based on these facts, the judge concluded:

"that the activity undertaken in respect of the property, again taken overall, was sufficient in nature and extent to amount to a business for the purpose of [incorporation relief]. Although each of the activities could equally well have been undertaken by someone who was a mere property investor, where the degree of activity outweighs what might normally be expected to be carried out by a mere passive investor, even a diligent and conscientious one, that will in my judgment amount to a business."

So, Mrs Ramsay qualified but the judge also made the point that another owner of investment property might only be a 'passive investor' who would not qualify and there was no single factor that determined this distinction: it was down to the degree of activity undertaken by the investor.

Hence, the danger for smaller landlords spending less than 20 hours per week on their business is that the business could be regarded as a 'passive investment'. Historically, HMRC has always taken the stance that 'the mere holding of investment property and collection of rent does not constitute a business' (while happily continuing to collect tax on income generated from this 'non-business' activity!)

But the helpful judge in the Ramsay case also gave us some factors that indicate when a business exists. He said one should consider whether there was/were:

i)   A serious undertaking earnestly pursued, or a serious occupation
ii)   An occupation or function actively pursued with reasonable or recognisable continuity
iii)   A certain amount of substance in terms of turnover
iv)   Activities conducted in a regular manner and on sound and recognised business principles
v)   Activities of a kind which, subject to differences of detail, are commonly made by those who seek to profit by them

Many smaller landlords would appear to meet most, if not all, of these tests and the idea that it is necessary to spend 20 hours per week on the business is not something that either the legislation or the judge ever actually said.

Nonetheless, attempting an incorporation relief claim if you spend less than 20 hours per week on your business could be risky. Sadly, HMRC will not give advance rulings on 'matters of fact, such as if certain activities constitute a business', so you will have no choice but to go ahead and then claim the relief on the basis you believe your business qualifies.

One of the major problems is that to get the relief, one must transfer the entire business to the company. If relief is not then forthcoming, there could be a substantial Capital Gains Tax bill.

Furthermore, whether relief is obtained or not, Stamp Duty Land Tax (or its equivalent in Scotland or Wales) will usually be payable on the market value of the properties transferred (subject to the partnership exemption and other available reliefs discussed above).

So, the stakes are high and, unless you clearly work an average of at least 20 hours per week in the business, the outcome will often be uncertain!

The Ramsay case is helpful, but it will be pretty rare for the property owner's circumstances to be exactly the same as Mrs Ramsay's. Hence, the question remains: how much more than passive investment does the business need to be in order to qualify?

Some of the key points that need to be considered after the Ramsay case are whether it is necessary for:

- The property to contain substantial communal areas
- The owner to carry out repairs and maintenance personally
- The property business to be the owner's only occupation
- The owner to be actively looking at ways to improve the capital value or rental yield of their property

Mrs Ramsay satisfied all these points. The position, where the property owner works less than 20 hours per week on their business, and only some of these points are satisfied, remains uncertain.

Some people are now arguing it is only necessary to satisfy the third point: that the business is the owner's only occupation. This is highly persuasive, but we do not agree that this can be seen as the single determining factor.

Nonetheless, there will be many cases where a property owner spending less than 20 hours per week on their business meets the standards set by the judge in the Ramsay case and qualifies for incorporation relief.

As always, we have to come back to the judge's comments in the case: is the activity undertaken, taken overall, sufficient to amount to a business? You might think so, but will the judge?

Is Now a Good Time to Transfer Property into a Company?

Earlier in this chapter, we discussed the fact that now may be a good time to transfer residential property into a company due to the temporary reduction in SDLT rates applying until 31st March 2021.

However, the sad fact is that there is another factor we should probably take into account: many properties' market values will have fallen significantly as a result of the coronavirus crisis.

While this is bad news overall, it does mean that the potential Capital Gains Tax and Stamp Duty Land Tax charges arising on a transfer of property into a company may be significantly reduced.

Example
Zoe and Yvonne are twin sisters and are both residential landlords. At the beginning of 2020, they each had a residential rental portfolio comprised of four properties with a total value of £1.6m. Each of them had acquired their properties for a total of £900,000 and thus had potential total capital gains of £700,000 on their portfolio.

The sisters are both higher rate taxpayers with another full-time job and they have both been advised they are unlikely to qualify for incorporation relief on a transfer of their properties into a company (we are making this point for the sake of illustration: in practice, we might not give up on this idea quite so easily).

In February 2020, Zoe decided that, despite the cost involved, she would transfer her properties into a company. Her total capital gains of £700,000 gave rise to a Capital Gains Tax bill of £192,640 (at 28%, after deducting her 2019/20 annual exemption of £12,000).

The company also had to pay Stamp Duty Land Tax at 'normal' rates (before the temporary reduction: see Chapter 23). It was, however, able to claim multiple dwellings relief and pay SDLT on the basis of the properties' average value of £400,000, thus reducing the SDLT bill to:

£125,000 x 3%   = £3,750
£125,000 x 5%   = £6,250
£150,000 x 8%   = £12,000
Total per property: £22,000
Total for four properties: £88,000 (£22,000 x 4)

The total tax cost of Zoe's transfer was thus £280,640 (£192,604 + £88,000).

Yvonne had been intending to follow suit and make a similar transfer of her portfolio into a company. However, due to the coronavirus crisis, her transfer was delayed. In the meantime, the reduced rates of SDLT had come into force and the market value of her properties had fallen by 15%, to a total of £1.36m, or an average of £340,000 per property.

Hence, when she finally came to make her transfer in September 2020, her total capital gain was £460,000 (£1.36m – £900,000), giving her a Capital Gains Tax bill of £125,356 (at 28%, after deducting her 2020/21 annual exemption of £12,300).

Her company's SDLT bill, after multiple dwellings relief, and using the reduced rates of SDLT now applying, was:

£340,000 x 3%= £10,200
Total per property: £10,200
Total for four properties: £40,800 (£10,200 x 4)

The total tax cost of Yvonne's transfer was thus £166,356 (£125,356 + £40,800), or £114,284 less than Zoe's transfer of an identical portfolio.

While the tax cost of Yvonne's transfer is still substantial (and, as the transfer took place after 5th April 2020, she will need to find the cash to pay it almost immediately), **she has saved well over £100,000**, by making the transfer under current conditions.

Part of that saving is due to a reduction in property values. The impact of that factor will vary from one landlord to another and none of us know when it will reverse.

But a large part of her saving is also due to the temporary reduction in SDLT rates, and we do know we only have until 31st March 2021 to benefit from this factor.

Hence, in summary, now may be the best possible time to transfer residential rental property into a company.

(With the possible exception of property in Scotland or Wales where, for the reasons explained earlier, a short delay may be sensible!)

Chapter 26

Using a Company: Mortgage Issues

Mortgages are available to company owners but the choice is fairly limited and the interest rates and arrangement fees may be higher.

In other words, some of what you gain from having full tax relief on your interest payments could be lost by paying a higher interest rate!

We asked Ray Boulger, senior mortgage technical manager at mortgage broker John Charcol, to comment on the market for company mortgages and are grateful for the following overview:

Although the choice of mortgages available on BTL properties owned by a company has increased significantly in recent years, many lenders still only offer a mortgage on properties owned in a personal name(s).

The increased competition from more lenders offering BTL mortgages to a company means that any individual lender will now often charge the same rate and fees as if the mortgage was in a personal name. However, because many lenders still do not offer a mortgage to a company the most competitive interest rates may not be available in a company name.

Lenders generally insist on purchasers using a separate special purpose vehicle (SPV), i.e. a company used solely for buy-to-let property and not allowed to conduct any other business activities. Some lenders are happy for an SPV to own more than one property, whereas others will only accept one property per SPV. Lenders nearly always insist on personal guarantees.

As far as existing properties are concerned, a personal borrower considering putting the property into a company would have to redeem any existing mortgage and apply for a new mortgage in the company's name. If their existing mortgage happened to be with one of the lenders offering mortgages to limited companies, it is probable the lender will help facilitate a smooth transfer to keep the business but a new application would have to be made and the interest rate may be different, as well as fees being incurred. However, major deterrents to transferring a property already owned into a limited company will often be not only the requirement to pay SDLT again (or similar in Scotland and Wales) as well as the SDLT surcharge, but also crystallisation of any CGT liability. There is also the risk of a lower valuation than previously obtained, which might result in a lower maximum loan being available or a higher interest rate being charged because the LTV is higher.

Because corporation tax is charged on the annual profit when a BTL property is held by a company, compared to the whole rental income being added to taxable income when held in a personal name, some lenders reflect this lower tax liability by applying a lower income cover requirement for interest cover, typically 125% instead of 145%. The effect of this is that it is sometimes possible to borrow more on properties held in a company name. Some lenders apply a lower stress test for the interest calculation on fixed rates of at least 5 years, for BTL mortgages in both personal and company names.

For large loans, whether on a single property or a portfolio, private banks will generally be happy to lend to SPVs, possibly at similar rates to personal customers. The commercial arms of some banks will also lend to SPVs, but normally charge more than their mortgage division would for a standard buy-to-let mortgage.

Portfolio Landlords

The Prudential Regulation Authority (PRA) now requires lenders to apply "specialist underwriting" to applications from landlords with four or more mortgaged properties, as a result of which some lenders no longer accept applications from these "portfolio landlords," although many will.

This specialist approach requires lenders to undertake a detailed review of a landlord's whole portfolio and business model and assess their ability to manage risk, but scope remains for lenders to apply the rules in different ways, particularly in the interest cover they require for the existing portfolio. For example, although a lender may require 145% rental cover on the new property being mortgaged it may accept 135% on the existing portfolio. Likewise some lenders require each individual property in a portfolio to pass its stress test but others only do so on a portfolio basis. Also lenders are allowed by the PRA to assume rent increases of up to 2% per annum.

156

As a result of the increased underwriting requirements lenders now require more information about the existing portfolio and may also ask for a business plan. For each property they will need its estimated value, rental income, mortgage amount and monthly payments. The extra work involved may lead to longer offer times but landlords can mitigate this by maintaining a spreadsheet with up to date information on their portfolio, so that all information required is readily available. This should also be helpful in managing their portfolio of properties and many portfolio landlords already maintain such records.

As the process of obtaining a new mortgage, including a remortgage, for portfolio landlords now requires more information to be provided to the lender it means more work for those landlords who don't maintain comprehensive accounting information for their portfolio.

Deeds of Trust/Beneficial Interest Trusts

In some cases, it may be possible to transfer the beneficial interest in properties to a company without disturbing the existing mortgage arrangements by using a Deed of Trust (also known as a Beneficial Interest Trust).

This will have the same consequences for both Capital Gains Tax and Stamp Duty Land Tax (or its equivalents in Scotland or Wales) as a transfer of the legal title.

This is a complex arrangement and we strongly recommend taking legal advice regarding the validity of the arrangement and the consequences regarding the outstanding mortgages. Our understanding is that it would be the property owner's legal obligation to ensure their mortgage lenders are fully advised of the arrangement. Furthermore, some lenders would not permit such an arrangement.

Chapter 27

Other Ways to Save Tax by Using a Company

In Chapters 24 and 25, we looked at the potential benefits of holding property in a company, as well as the many complexities involved in transferring property to a company.

There may, however, be other ways to save tax by using a company that do not involve the company actually owning any property.

Leasing Property to Your Own Company

You can reduce the amount of tax you pay personally by leasing property to your own company, which will then rent the property to your tenants.

This could be a useful means to avoid exposure to higher rate tax on profits you are not actually making.

Example

Margaret has a salary of £40,000 and a small portfolio of rental property yielding total gross rental income of £25,000. She pays mortgage interest on her rental properties totalling £10,000 and other annual costs of £5,000, giving her a true rental profit of £10,000.

This year (2020/21) Margaret's taxable rental profit will be £20,000 (£25,000 - £5,000), of which £10,000 will fall into her basic rate band and get taxed at 20% and £10,000 will be taxed at 40%. Her tax liability therefore totals £6,000.

Margaret can then claim a tax reduction of £2,000 (£10,000 x 20%) in respect of her mortgage interest, leaving her with a net tax bill of £4,000 and after tax income from her property business of £6,000.

Instead of this, however, Margaret leases her properties to her company for £10,500 per year. She still pays the same amount of mortgage interest but her annual costs fall to just £500, leaving her in a 'true' position of break even.

Her taxable rental profit will now be £10,000 (£10,500 - £500) which will all be taxed at basic rate, meaning that her tax reduction for mortgage interest will leave her with no tax to pay overall.

The company makes a rental profit of £10,000 (£25,000 rent received less lease payments of £10,500 and the remaining £4,500 of annual costs). After paying Corporation Tax at 19%, it is left with an after tax profit of £8,100.

Margaret can take up to £2,000 of the company's after tax profit as a tax-free dividend but will suffer Income Tax at 32.5% on any excess.

She will therefore be left with total after tax income between £6,117 and £8,100, depending on how much she retains within the company. However, if she extracts all her company profits, she will be just £117 better off overall.

This arrangement has some potential drawbacks. There will be significant legal and professional costs involved, which will outweigh an annual saving of just £117 (but could be worthwhile on a bigger scale).

Normally, if the lease to the company is for a long enough period to have a 'net present value' in excess of £125,000, Stamp Duty Land Tax will be payable at 1% on the excess. However, this threshold has temporarily been increased to £500,000 for new leases granted between 8th July 2020 and 31st March 2021. Hence, once again, now may be a good time to undertake this type of planning.

See the Taxcafe.co.uk guide *'How to Save Property Tax'* for further details regarding SDLT on leases.

The charges under the lease must not exceed a normal, commercial 'arm's length' rate. However, it appears there is no problem with them being lower.

Lastly, it may be necessary to get the mortgage lender's permission for the arrangement and this will not always be forthcoming. Legal advice is again essential.

Using a Property Management Company

In Chapter 14, we looked at the possibility of reducing the taxable profits on your property business by paying management fees to some form of connected entity. We expressed some reservations regarding this arrangement and stressed the importance for it to have an appropriate level of commercial substance.

Subject to these reservations (and the two 'words of warning' we also emphasised), it is possible for a landlord to use a property management company to reduce their own tax burden.

Example
Carter is an additional rate taxpayer with a large property portfolio generating annual gross rents of £400,000. In 2020/21, he decides to sub-contract the management of his properties to a new property management company, Danco Property Services Limited.

Danco Property Services Limited charges Carter 15% of the gross annual rents on the properties (£60,000) as a service charge for managing the portfolio. Naturally, the company also ends up bearing some of the expenses in running the property portfolio and these amount to £6,000.

Carter's taxable income will now be reduced by £54,000 (£60,000 - £6,000), saving him £24,300 in Income Tax (at 45%). Meanwhile, Danco Property Services Limited will have annual profits of £54,000, giving it a Corporation Tax bill, at 19%, of £10,260.

The overall tax paid by Carter and Danco Property Services Limited combined is thus reduced by £14,040 (£24,300 - £10,260).

As usual, however, it doesn't work quite so well if the company's profits are extracted. If Carter takes out all the company's after-tax profit of £43,740 as a dividend, he will pay additional Income Tax of £15,903:

£43,740 less £2,000 dividend allowance = £41,740 x 38.1% = £15,903

*This turns the £14,040 saving into an overall additional tax **cost** of £1,863!*

For Carter to be able to claim a valid Income Tax deduction for the company's management fees, he must be able to show they were incurred wholly and exclusively for the benefit of his property rental business. In other words, there must be a genuine provision of services by the company.

Furthermore, as explained in Chapter 14, this type of arrangement is only likely to be valid where the property management company has other unconnected clients.

This, in turn, may create another problem: if the total level of management fees (and other charges, commission, or sales) charged by the company exceeds the VAT registration threshold, it will need to register for and charge VAT at 20%.

If, as will generally be the case, the individual landlord is unable to recover this VAT, it will completely undo the whole purpose of the exercise and could turn it into a costly mess!

Example continued
Danco Property Services Limited has a number of other clients and the fees charged to Carter take its total gross income over the VAT registration threshold. It therefore has to start charging VAT at 20%.

Carter now pays management fees totalling £72,000 (£60,000 + 20%), so his taxable income is reduced by £66,000 (£72,000 - £6,000) and his Income Tax bill reduces by £29,700 (£66,000 x 45%).

The company is now able to recover £1,000 of input VAT included within its annual costs of £6,000, so the net amount of VAT paid over to HM Revenue and Customs in respect of its contract with Carter is £11,000 (£60,000 x 20% = £12,000 – £1,000 = £11,000).

The company's taxable profit on its contract with Carter is now £55,000 (£1,000 more than before due to the recovery of input VAT), giving it a Corporation Tax bill, at 19%, of £10,450.

The overall net position is now as follows:

Income tax saved by Carter:	*£29,700*
Less:	
VAT paid by company:	*£11,000*
Corporation tax paid by company:	*£10,450*
Equals a net saving of:	*£8,250*

*BUT, this net saving is reliant on Carter leaving after tax profits of £44,550 in the company. If he takes these out as a dividend, he will pay a further £16,212 in Income Tax and there will be an overall tax **cost** of £7,962!*

As we can see, using your own property management company carries a number of potential pitfalls and, done badly, could end up costing a great deal of extra tax.

However, subject to all our reservations, and most especially our 'words of warning' in Chapter 14, if done well it could save a significant amount of tax.

Doing it 'well' will include reinvesting some or all of the company's after tax profits within the company and managing the company's business carefully so that, while it does take on other, unconnected clients, its total gross income remains below the VAT registration threshold.

Furthermore, if you manage to do it 'well', even greater tax savings may be possible if the company is owned by and/or employs your spouse, partner or other family members.

Chapter 28

The Cash Basis for Landlords

Most unincorporated property businesses (i.e. individual landlords) can now use the "cash basis" to calculate their tax.

The cash basis is open to landlords with total gross annual rental income (before deducting **any** expenses) of £150,000 or less.

Those who use the cash basis only pay tax on the rental income they've actually *received* during the year. If a tenant should have paid rent but hasn't, it is not taxable. By the same token, landlords are only able to claim tax relief for expenses they've actually *paid* during the year.

By contrast, under traditional 'accruals basis' accounting (also know as GAAP accounting) income is included when it is earned, even if it hasn't been received yet, and expenses are included when they are incurred, even if they haven't been paid yet. (A bad debt expense may, of course, eventually be claimed where it becomes unlikely that income which was due will ever be received.)

Note that the cash basis is now the **default** method landlords must use to calculate their tax, unless they opt out, or their gross rental income for the year exceeds £150,000. If they opt out, they can use traditional 'accruals basis' accounting instead.

Landlords who would otherwise fall into the cash basis must make the election to opt out every year when they complete their tax returns.

Partnerships can use the cash basis as long as all the partners are individuals. Companies, trusts, limited liability partnerships, and partnerships with one or more corporate partners are excluded.

For the purposes of both the £150,000 threshold, and the question of whether you wish to opt out of the cash basis, UK and overseas properties are, as usual, regarded as separate businesses. Hence, you could have £100,000 of gross annual rental income from UK property and £100,000 of gross annual rental income from overseas property and still be eligible for the cash basis for both businesses. Furthermore, you could, if you wish, opt out of the cash basis for one of those businesses but remain in the cash basis for the other.

If the landlord also has a separate trading business, a separate decision (whether or not to use the cash basis) can be taken for the trading and property businesses.

Where you own any rental property jointly with another person, you must both use the same basis (i.e. either the 'cash basis' or the 'accruals basis') for the relevant property business (UK or overseas). This means many landlords with joint interests in property are unable to use the cash basis.

Transitional rules apply in the year a landlord enters or leaves the cash basis. Broadly speaking, these rules are designed to ensure that all income is taxed once, but only once, and all qualifying expenses are relieved once, but only once.

Timing Issues

Generally speaking, where a landlord has the same marginal tax rate each year, it usually makes sense to defer taxable income and accelerate deductible expenditure wherever possible. Hence, under normal circumstances, the cash basis will generally be disadvantageous for landlords because, under the cash basis:

- Rent becomes fully taxable on receipt, even if it relates to a period that extends beyond the end of the tax year

- Expenses that have been incurred but not yet paid at the end of the tax year cannot be claimed

However, for the same reasons, the cash basis may prove advantageous in some cases. If the landlord expects their marginal tax rate to increase in a future tax year, accelerating taxable income, or deferring deductible expenditure, may lead to considerable tax savings.

Furthermore, the cash basis opens up more opportunities to defer deductible expenditure. For example, allowable repairs expenditure could be carried out during one tax year, but paid for in a later year when the landlord has a higher marginal tax rate.

As discussed in Chapter 12, some expenditure is related to a specific time period and hence, under traditional 'accruals basis' accounting, will generally have to be claimed as an expense of that period. Under the cash basis, however, a landlord could delay paying things like ground rent and utility bills for a short period so they may be claimed in a later year when the landlord has a higher marginal tax rate. Changing the payment of insurance premiums from a single payment to a monthly direct debit could also have a similar beneficial effect.

Naturally, it is generally only possible to delay payments for a short period and the impact on your relationship with the payees needs to be considered.

Finance Costs under the Cash Basis

Under the different cash basis for *trading* businesses, a deduction of no more than £500 is allowed for interest expenses on cash borrowings. Under the cash basis for *property* businesses, there is a different restriction (see below) but it only applies in limited circumstances.

Thus most landlords who decide to use the cash basis will be able to claim all their finance costs (including loan arrangement fees) *as they are paid*, subject to the tax relief restriction that is the focus of this guide. (Adding arrangement fees to the loan counts as *paid* for this purpose.)

By contrast, under traditional 'accruals basis' accounting, loan arrangement fees generally cannot be claimed in one go in the year they are paid and have to be spread over several years (see Chapter 15). From 2020/21 onwards, these costs only attract tax relief at 20%.

Thus, landlords who paid loan arrangement fees last year (2019/20), and use the cash basis when they submit their 2019/20 tax returns, may be able to enjoy more tax relief than landlords who use traditional 'accruals basis' accounting.

For a typical higher-rate taxpayer with a marginal tax rate of 40%, the effective rate of relief for their finance costs during the 2019/20 tax year was 25%.

For example, if you are a higher-rate taxpayer and incurred mortgage arrangement fees of £10,000 in 2019/20, you will enjoy tax relief of £2,500 under the cash basis (£10,000 x 25%). Under traditional 'accruals basis' accounting, this cost would generally have to be spread over several years, and most of it would therefore attract tax relief at just 20%.

Furthermore, as explained in Chapter 15, it's not too late to amend your 2018/19 tax return and use the cash basis for that year as well. For a typical higher-rate taxpayer with a marginal tax rate of 40%, the effective rate of relief for their finance costs during the 2018/19 tax year was 30%.

Hence, for example, if you were a higher-rate taxpayer in 2018/19 and incurred mortgage arrangement fees of £10,000 that year, you could enjoy tax relief of £3,000 if you amended your tax return to use the cash basis (you have until 31st January 2021 to make such an amendment).

The tax and accounting treatment applying to loan arrangement fees also extends to professional and other costs associated with obtaining long-term loan finance (including mortgages). For further details see the Taxcafe.co.uk guide 'How to Save Property Tax'.

Tax Relief Restrictions under the Cash Basis

Generally speaking, using the cash basis only alters the timing of when expenses may be claimed for tax purposes (i.e. changing it from when the expense is *incurred*, to when it is *paid*). However, there are a few circumstances under which the *total* amount of expenses claimed may be restricted under the cash basis.

Firstly, there is a further restriction on interest relief where additional borrowings are taken out for business purposes and these additional borrowings take the total amount borrowed to fund the landlord's property business beyond the total of all their rental properties' original values when first rented out (plus any subsequent capital improvement expenditure on the properties).

Secondly, there are some restrictions on capital expenses: i.e. the cost of assets purchased for use in the business, or other costs relating to those purchases. Relief for this type of expenditure is also restricted under traditional 'accruals basis' accounting, but there are additional restrictions under the cash basis. The most important of these **additional** restrictions for landlords to be aware of, are:

- Abortive expenditure (e.g. legal fees or survey fees) relating to potential purchases of new property that are abandoned is not allowable under the cash basis. Such expenses should normally be allowable under traditional 'accruals basis' accounting, provided a final decision to purchase the property had not yet been made at the time the expense was incurred.

- No deductions are allowed in respect of lease premiums paid by landlords operating under the cash basis.

- 'Integral features' and other property fixtures that might normally qualify for capital allowances under traditional 'accruals basis' accounting cannot be claimed under the cash basis when these form part of a property's purchase cost. Additional fixtures added to a property later may, however, qualify, and replacements will, of course, usually be correctly classed as repairs and not as capital expenditure. (This restriction will mostly only affect landlords purchasing commercial property or furnished holiday lets, although it may also affect some residential property purchases where the property is divided into a number of self-contained flats.)

See the Taxcafe.co.uk guide *'How to Save Property Tax'* for further details of the impact of these restrictions and the treatment of all types of capital expenses mentioned above under both traditional 'accruals basis' accounting and the cash basis.

Comparing Cash and Accruals

To further illustrate some of the points outlined above let's take a look at an example.

Example
Safiya is a full-time residential landlord with no other sources of income. During the 2020/21 tax year, she receives rent totalling £100,000, pays interest of £40,000 and incurs other expenses of £20,000, including £2,500 in professional fees in respect of potential new properties she later decided not to buy and £7,500 for some roof repairs carried out in March 2021, which she pays in late April.

The total value of her properties when they were each rented out for the first time was £900,000, but her borrowings now total £1 million. It is beyond doubt that all her borrowings were for purely business reasons. Nonetheless, this still means that, under the cash basis, she can only claim 90% of her interest cost (£900,000/£1m = 90%).

£12,000 of Safiya's income was received in the first five days of April 2021 and relates to the rent due for the whole of that month.

Safiya's accountant works out her profit under traditional 'accruals basis' accounting as follows:

Income due for the year	*£90,000*
(£100,000 – £12,000 x 25/30)	
Less expenses:	
Interest	*£40,000*
Other expenses incurred	*£20,000*
Accrued accountancy fees	*£2,000*
Rental profit	*£28,000*

Safiya's interest expense will be added back to her profit for tax purposes and will instead give rise to a tax deduction at basic rate.

If Safiya does not elect to use traditional 'accruals basis' accounting, she will fall into the cash basis by default and her rental income will then be calculated as follows:

Income received in the year	*£100,000*
Less expenses paid in the year:	
Interest (£40,000 x 90%)	*£36,000*
Other (£12,500 paid, less professional fees not allowed £2,500)	*£10,000*
Net rental income	*£54,000*

Safiya's allowable interest payments will be added to her income for tax purposes and will instead give rise to a tax deduction at basic rate.

As we can see, the cash basis would cause a considerable increase in Safiya's tax liability for 2020/21. Her taxable rental income will increase from £68,000 (£28,000 + £40,000) to £90,000 (£54,000 + £36,000), costing her an extra £8,800 in Income Tax (£22,000 x 40%). Her interest eligible for a tax reduction at basic rate will also be reduced from £40,000 to £36,000, losing her a further £800 in tax relief. Overall, her tax bill is increased by £9,600.

However, it is worth pointing out that the £22,000 increase in her taxable income is made up of a number of elements, some of which are only timing differences that will reverse in a later year, and some of which are 'absolute' – i.e. a loss of relief that will not reverse. These can be summarised as follows:

Timing differences	
Rental income accelerated	*£10,000*
Unpaid repair bill	*£7,500*
Accrued accountancy fees	*£2,000*
Total	*£19,500*
Absolute differences	
Abortive professional fees	*£2,500*

She has also lost out on a tax reduction for a further £4,000 of disallowed interest.

Let us now suppose the timing differences will reverse the following year when Safiya's marginal tax rate is 60% (i.e. her total taxable income is between £100,000 and £125,000: see Chapter 12 for a further explanation of the marginal rate arising).

The reversal of her timing differences could result in a tax saving for 2021/22 of up to £11,700 (£19,500 x 60%).

However, Safiya will again lose out on tax relief for £4,000 of her interest cost, giving rise to additional Income Tax of £800 (£4,000 x 20%).

Her net saving for 2021/22 is thus £10,900 (£11,700 – £800) and hence, overall, between the two years, Safiya has saved £1,300 (£10,900 – £9,600).

BUT, instead of using the cash basis in 2021/22, Safiya could opt out and return to traditional 'accruals basis' accounting. The transitional rules would ensure her timing differences of £19,500 reversed, but the additional restriction on her interest expenses would no longer apply. Hence, the additional cost of £9,600 in 2020/21 would be significantly outweighed by an £11,700 saving in 2021/22, and Safiya would be £2,100 better off overall.

As we can see, switching between traditional 'accruals basis' accounting and the cash basis may provide another mechanism to effectively accelerate taxable income into a year when the landlord has a lower marginal tax rate; and defer deductible expenditure to a year when they have a higher marginal tax rate: thus producing overall savings.

However, in some cases, this will come at a cost, with potential 'absolute' losses of tax relief on some expenses. This is something landlords need to factor into their considerations when deciding whether to use the cash basis.

The Cash Basis and the Coronavirus Crisis

In the above example, we assumed Safiya was moving from being a normal, typical, higher rate taxpayer with a marginal tax rate of 40% in 2020/21, to being in the £100,000 to £125,000 taxable income bracket, with a marginal tax rate of 60%, in 2021/22. This could happen for a variety of reasons, but it may have been because Safiya's income was reduced in 2020/21 due to the coronavirus crisis.

Reduced rental income in 2020/21 could happen for a number of reasons, including voids and rent arrears.

As far as voids are concerned, this reduces the amount of rental income both *received* and *receivable*. Hence, broadly speaking, the impact will be the same whether the landlord uses traditional 'accruals basis' accounting or the cash basis.

The question with rent arrears is whether these are eventually paid late, or not at all. Under traditional 'accruals basis' accounting, the rent arrears remain part of the landlord's *receivable* income and, in principle, continue to be taxable income: although the landlord can claim a bad debt expense in respect of the arrears when they are able to make a reasonable judgement that they are not likely to be paid.

Under the cash basis, of course, the landlord is only taxed on rent actually *received*, meaning that tax relief for bad debts is automatic and rent paid late is only taxed when the cash actually comes in. From a cashflow perspective, therefore, the cash basis will almost always be more beneficial when the landlord has significant rent arrears.

Example

Angela has a portfolio of residential rental properties producing total annual rent receivable of £100,000. At 5th April 2020, all her tenants were up to date with their rent.

During 2020/21, several of her tenants ran into financial difficulties as a result of the coronavirus crisis. At 5th April 2021, Angela had rent arrears totalling £40,000. In other words, the rent she actually received during 2020/21 was just £60,000. If she uses the cash basis, she will obviously only pay tax on this amount for 2020/21.

By the time Angela is preparing her 2020/21 accounts and tax return (in December 2021), the position with the rent arrears that were outstanding at 5th April 2021 is as follows:

Received	*£10,000*
Forgiven*	*£5,000*
Arrangements in hand for payment to be made over an agreed period	*£17,000*
Tenants made redundant and unable to pay	*£8,000*

* Rent 'forgiven' represents amounts Angela has agreed may be waived. This effectively reduces her rent receivable for 2020/21 and will

therefore produce tax relief under either traditional 'accruals basis' accounting or the cash basis.

If Angela uses traditional 'accruals basis' accounting, she will have to include the £10,000 of arrears that have now been received in her taxable income for 2020/21. However, she may claim a bad debt expense for the £8,000 that she is now unlikely to ever receive.

The £17,000 being paid over an agreed period is the most difficult part to assess under traditional 'accruals basis' accounting. Angela will need to make a reasonable judgement regarding how much of this sum is likely to be recovered and include those recoverable elements within her taxable income for 2020/21. Depending on the circumstances, she is likely to have to include somewhere between 50% and 90% of this income in 2020/21. She will also have to continue to assess how much of this income remains recoverable in each subsequent tax return until all of the arrears have either been recovered, or she can reasonably assume they will never be received.

Hence, in summary, under the cash basis, Angela will be taxed on rent received of £60,000 in 2020/21.

Under traditional 'accruals basis' accounting, she will be taxed on rent receivable of somewhere between £78,500 (£60,000 + £10,000 + £17,000 x 50%) and £85,300 (£60,000 + £10,000 + £17,000 x 90%).

In other words, the cash basis will defer between £18,500 and £25,300 of Angela's taxable income into a later tax year.

Assuming Angela is a typical higher rate taxpayer with a marginal tax rate of 40% in 2020/21, using the cash basis will give her a tax saving of between £7,400 and £10,120 for this year.

In cashflow terms this is obviously extremely beneficial. The only question is: will she have a higher marginal tax rate when this timing difference reverses in 2021/22 and later years? If so, she may end up paying more tax overall in the end, and that is something she will need to weigh up when she is deciding whether to use the cash basis.

See the Taxcafe.co.uk guide *'How to Save Property Tax'* for a more detailed examination of when it is reasonable for landlords to claim bad debt expenses under traditional 'accruals basis' accounting and how to assess the proper amount to claim.

The Cash Basis and Rent Arrears

To summarise the position regarding rent arrears under the cash basis:

- The overall position is much simpler as the landlord only has to account for rent actually received in the tax year
- Relief for bad debts is automatic and does not require the landlord to assess the position and justify their stance
- Tax is deferred on other arrears, which are eventually received
- Significant cashflow savings may arise
- However, it is important to consider whether there may eventually be an overall additional cost where the landlord's marginal tax rate is likely to be higher in future tax years

Lightning Source UK Ltd.
Milton Keynes UK
UKHW021006160720
366641UK00006B/159